Praise for

UNBREAKABLE.
UNSTOPPABLE.
AN AMERICAN SOLDIER'S STORY
OF
COMING HOME

"I truly enjoyed reading your book! I couldn't put it down. Your authenticity showed. You have a great sense of humor, you are brave, and you have an intrepid spirit. Your book will have a profound effect on civilians and veterans alike both in understanding things like "the horrors of the hospital and recovery are sometimes worse than the horrors on the battlefield" and all the other B.S. you and many others like you, have risen above."

—Faye Nelson
Executive Director, Warriors & Quiet Waters

"From Unbreakable, Unstoppable: An American Soldier's Story of Coming Home, one suspects there is a sort of symbiotic relationship between the US Army paratroops attracting a tougher-than-average person and the airborne units forging a more resilient man from uncommon stock. Jose Navarro's story is Ron Kovic's Born on the Fourth of July, but more powerful, more inspirational, and more compelling in every sense. It speaks directly to the experience of the post-9/11 veteran and their families and loved ones. Whereas Kovic was the all-American kid from middle America, young Jose narrowly escapes the 'hood and a life of gang-banging' by enlisting in the Army. There he finds dignity, a future, and the family he never had in the brotherhood of the legendary 82nd Airborne Division, only to lose it all in a Taliban ambush in Afghanistan. He survives seven subsequent years of hospitalization only by mastering adversity, continually seeking redemption, and forgiving the soldier whose cowardice led to Jose's catastrophic injuries."

—Michael J.MacLeod
Author of *The Brave Ones: A Memoir of Hope, Pride, and Military Service*

More praise for

UNBREAKABLE.
UNSTOPPABLE.
AN AMERICAN SOLDIER'S STORY
OF
COMING HOME

"When Jose shared a few chapters of his book with me I was taken by his willingness to bare his sufferings to the world of such a personal nature and do it with such honesty. I had never read such a heartfelt story. I feel it important for the civilian world to know the sufferings of our young men and women. Jose has shown me the strength of a true warrior, perhaps having private times of total despair, but never showing them to the outside world. Jose showed me such fortitude during this journey. I feel his story should be shared as it will be an inspiration to others who suffer wounds of war."

—Maggie Lockridge RN, Veteran USAFNC
President/Founder, Rebuilding America's Warriors (RAW) Foundation

UNBREAKABLE.
UNSTOPPABLE.

AN AMERICAN SOLDIER'S STORY
OF
COMING HOME

Jose Francisco Navarro

Cover Design by Sloane McCue, PFL.com
Book design and production by PFL
www.pfl.com

DEDICATION

This book is dedicated to the brave men of the 4th Squadron, 73rd Cavalry Regiment, 82nd Airborne Division.

- Sgt. Zachary D. Tellier
- Pfc. Jordan E. Goode
- Sgt. Tyler Juden

Until Valhalla, Brothers…

ACKNOWLEDGMENTS

There are a number of people I want to thank for helping me bring this book forward.

Warriors & Quiet Waters. Thank you for my two FX's, then for the Coaching FX, and now with your support for getting this book distributed to the people who need it most.

PFL. Thank you for making the publication of this book possible by printing it and taking such care. Thank you also for your patience in allowing me to complete all the stories I needed to without pressure.

Mike MacLeod. Thank you for first sitting down with me and talking about telling my story. You gave me the first outline of what to consider including, and that started me off in the right direction.

Ris Higgins. Wow, what an enlightening, hilarious, and embarrassing experience this has been. Thank you for your patience and understanding. I'm glad I was able to add to your vocabulary! You are more than my editor and coach; you are my friend.

CONTENTS

Note: The stories in this book are true, but many names have been changed to protect the privacy of individuals.

FOREWORD

I just read an excerpt from the rough draft of Jose Navarro's book, *Unbreakable. Unstoppable. An American Soldier's Story of Coming Home.* To say that I am blown away by the power of his writing is an understatement. His story is one that must be read by anyone who blithely agrees to send our brave young men into battle a world away from home without being aware of the consequences of that action. The casualties of war are clearly and devastatingly brought to life by his story. These are not simply a black and white number of combat deaths or wounded; they're the personal tragedies that are too easily overlooked amongst the cold statistics. Jose's story tells it as it is.

I have been honored to be the medical director of the Rebuilding America's Warriors (RAW) Foundation since its inception in 2007. During that time I have seen many veterans whose lives were changed, and in some cases, devastated by their combat-sustained wounds. Some of these wounds run deeper than others, inflicting severe damage not only upon the physical body but also to the emotional stability of the individual.

When Jose first came to see me, he had already gone through perhaps 100 operations at Walter Reed and other US Army facilities. His injuries were not so obvious to the onlooker as they may have been. He had all his arms and legs and no visible damage to his head and neck. His wounds were all below the waist; an explosion destroyed his groin and pelvic areas. His genitalia were essentially gone, along with severe tissue loss to his thighs and buttocks. These are not the type of injuries that people are comfortable discussing. The fact that Jose is brave enough to write openly about it is just another measure of his strength.

Jose had undergone many procedures to try to reconstruct his genitalia. Overlooking for the moment the physical travails involved in successfully undergoing these surgeries, the embarrassment and feelings of loss of masculinity that he experienced led to years of depression, prescription drug dependency, and feelings of isolation, anger, and inadequacy.

When I first met Jose, he was standing up in my exam room. He told me he preferred to stand rather than sit in my exam chair. This was because the wounds and reconstructive procedures had left him with no soft tissue padding over his iliac tuberosities, the"sit-bones." The most difficult chairs for him were the hard plastic ones that are so prevalent at most governmental facilities. The pressure on his unprotected bones and nerves was intolerable.

I worked with Jose to surgically build up the soft tissue layers over his bones, mostly using fat grafting from elsewhere on his body. I wasn't sure how much improvement I could give him, but we both hoped for the best. When he came back to see me several weeks after the operation, he was sitting in the chair when I walked into the exam room, a definite successful outcome.

The reconstruction of his genitalia was a different story. Working with Maggie Lockridge, the founder of the RAW Foundation, we got Jose a referral to Dr. Gary Alter, a colleague of mine in Beverly Hills who is a board certified plastic surgeon and urologist. Dr. Alter helped Jose a great deal and then made a referral to one of the outstanding urogenital practices in the country in Virginia.

Jose's success is not simply measured by his physical rehabilitation. It is much more amply demonstrated by his return to civilian life, with friends and family. He is a brave man who has triumphed over adversities that most of us cannot even comprehend.

Way to go, Jose!

Dr. Norman Leaf, MD, FACS
Clinical Associate Professor Department of Plastic Surgery
UCLA Medical School

PREFACE

My name is Jose Francisco Navarro. I have had many adventures in life. I have endured many hardships and reaped the benefits of having overcome them. I wrote this book to show people that no situation is hopeless. Your worst nightmare can be conquered through love and faith.

Life is full of the unexpected. Often times we feel defeated, trapped, alone, and unloved. These are only feelings, not facts. No matter the circumstances, no matter the pain and heartache, we have the power to adapt and overcome any trial life has in store for us.

Here's what I've learned. We all own the ability to love ourselves. Nothing, or no one, can ever take that from us. Once we learn to love ourselves, anything is possible. Love will find you. Love doesn't need to be searched for. Our lives have value, meaning, and purpose beyond our understanding. However, it's up to us to manifest the outcome.

CHILDHOOD

I was born and raised in Pomona California, an only child to Elizabeth and Jose Navarro. My fondest childhood memories are of my mother picking me up from school so we could have lunch together. She would drop me off at my grandmother's house so I could play with my uncles and aunts who were only a few years older than me until she returned from work.

My home was a different story. My father was an alcoholic, womanizing drug addict. As a child, I was afraid of him. As soon as he came home from work, I would find someplace to hide or go outside with my pitbull, Rufus. I hid because that's when the arguments would start. I avoided him because he would always treat me as if I was in the way. At a young age, I was embarrassed by him.

Still, I wanted to be like him. He was the life of the party, a master BBQ chef and an intelligent, successful man. He was a top electrical mechanic making well over $85,000 in the early '90s. My father had it all: a beautiful wife, a son, a champion pit bull, a house, a boat, and multiple cars. My favorite was a beautifully restored 1955 Chevy Bel Air. It was a family heirloom given to my father by his grandmother. As a child,
I would sneak into the garage and pretend to drive it. I hoped that one day he would show me how to work on cars and hand down the 55
Bel Air to me.

My mother would always leave him about every six months or so. I loved when this happened because we would go stay with my grandparents or sometimes we would get a place of our own. There were no arguments then. I wasn't afraid to come home, and I always had friends and family over. It's when I had my mother all to myself.

5

My mother had a strict Mexican Catholic upbringing where divorce was a sin, so she did everything in her power to make it work. She would always end up going back to my father, and things would still go the same way. The drinking and drugs would stop for a few months, then start back up again along with the misery and fear.

She managed two doctors' offices. One of the doctors she worked for noticed something was wrong when my father would call her at work obsessively. Sometimes he showed up drunk at her work in an attempt to intimidate anyone who showed interest in her. The doctor was also sexually harassing her.

Years of neglect, dysfunction, and my father's infidelity, along with drug and alcohol abuse, had taken a toll on my naïve mother. The stress of work, the burden of having to raise me alone, my father's lifestyle, and an abusive marriage became too much to handle. My mother had a nervous breakdown and fell into a deep depression.

She came home from work one day, went to the backyard with my father, and began drinking with him. I found this odd because we had just moved back in with him because he completed a sobriety course of some kind.

They spent weeks together drinking excessively and arguing. The funny thing was, none of this was abnormal to me.

Then I noticed that my mother was not getting out of bed or going to work. She stopped eating, and every time I went into her room, she was crying. When she asked me if I wanted to stay at my Grandma Navarro's house, I jumped for joy. I was the only male grandchild on that side of the family, so I was spoiled by everyone there. I moved in with my grandparents and my Aunt Mary. I still did not see anything wrong with this picture.

Living at my grandmother's house was one of the loneliest times of my life. I had a lot of attention, but I was without my mother. I did not hear from her for weeks, so my Aunt Mary looked after me most of the time. I was stuck to her like glue, afraid she would leave me. I remember going shopping with her and pissing myself because I was scared that if I went to the restroom, she wouldn't be there when I got out.

School was changing for me as well. I used to be the class clown, a popular kid. Now I was depressed all the time. Sometimes I would cry in class which provoked kids who were once my friends to pick on me. Children can be vicious creatures. One time I got punched in the face in class while sitting at my desk for no reason. I started to get into multiple fights a week. I was only in the fourth grade, and I hated school.

I moved back with my mother and father. They had moved out of our house into a small ghetto ass trailer. It was in front of a railroad track down the street from a strip club located on the street known as the "Hoe Stroll." At any given time there would be up to 30 prostitutes on the corner. The trailer park's occupants were mostly Mexican day laborers and crackheads.

My parent's condition became worse because both of them were not working. My mother was in a deep depression—she had turned into skin and bones, she was always crying, and she never got out of bed. My father's drug and alcohol abuse had gotten worse, as did his behavior. There were always arguments, and there was never any food. I hated being home.

As odd as this may sound, I had some of my best childhood memories in that trailer park. There were a lot of boys around my age. They were the sons of crackheads, prostitutes, and illegal immigrants. We would spend the day riding our bikes around town, vandalizing property, and throwing rocks at the railroad crackheads. We accumulated a sweet porn collection.

We also loved to steal from the local liquor store. It got so bad that the store owner placed a sign in the window that said, "only one kid in at a time."

I did whatever I could not to go back home. There was a negative presence there. My parents were in their own fucked up world, and I was not a part of it. I was heartbroken for my mother, and I was afraid of my father. We lived this way for about two years.

My father continued the cycle of rehab, stopping the drugs and alcohol for a few months, then starting back up again. One time we actually thought he had changed. Things were getting better, so my mother returned to work, and she began to regain her weight.

One day I found his work shed unlocked and found hundreds of vodka bottles. He had been drinking behind our backs the whole time. Angry and heartbroken, I snitched on him as soon as my mom got home. She went into a fit of rage and broke every bottle that was there. It looked like a trailer trash scene from the show, "Cops."

That was the final breaking point. My mother and I moved out, and she divorced my father. I was so happy because I thought from now on it was going to be just her and me. We got an apartment, but we received no child support payments nor had any support from our family. My father's family kicked me to the curb, and my mother's family was absent.

My mother now had the burden of paying the bills and raising a son by herself. She changed. She was no longer the mother I knew; she was always angry. If I did any little thing to upset her, I was quickly corrected with the wire hanger. She would punish me with yearlong punishments and would follow through.

We were dead broke. My dinner every night was a 99 cent Whopper from Burger King. If I wanted cheese, I would have to come up with 35 cents for "cheese money." Sometimes when I couldn't come up with the money, I would try to sneak the cheese into my order. If the bill came out to more than $1.07, my mother took the burger back and made them take the cheese off. She whipped the shit out of me when we got home. I hated her for that, but little did I know she was eating oatmeal for breakfast, lunch, and dinner. This is what my mother and I had to do to get by.

My world did not turn out the way I thought it would. My mother was young and beautiful; she got the attention of men everywhere we went. I would try to look tough and try to intimidate grown men who would hit on her.

My mother would work all day, and as soon as she got home, she would get on the phone and lock herself in her room. On the weekends she went out, and all I wanted was her time. She was my world, and she chose to ignore me.

My mother was always angry, and she made me pay for her anger. She chose to live her own life rather than own up to her responsibilities as a mother. Her boyfriends were pretty much my dad without the drugs and alcohol. I could not understand why she would rather spend time with them instead of me. I felt she was angry that she had to take care of me, and if I wasn't in the picture, she would be free to live her life. I began to hate her.

TEEN YEARS

At a young age, I quickly learned the value of a dollar. My mother could not afford new clothes, shoes, or toys for me. I would wear the same clothes over and over to school which did not add to my cool factor.

Most kids ate fruit loops and drank Kool-Aid. I ate fruit rings and drank flavor aid. If my pants were faded, I had to dye them. If I wanted something, I would have to come up with a way to get it myself. It taught me how to save and manage money well. I was determined to have the things my father never gave me. I bought my own Schwinn bicycles and learned to restore them. I bought my own barbecue grill and taught myself how to barbecue through trial and error.

As a child, I always had a hustle of some kind. One summer I charged neighbors to kill wasp nests outside their houses. I did this with a long stick nailed to a bean can filled with poison. I started working as soon as I was able to at 15½.

At 14 I realized my mother couldn't hurt me anymore. She was wrong. I could do whatever I wanted, and she wouldn't care because she hated me.

I was always in the streets because it was the only place I felt free. In the streets, I met kids whom I could relate to, most of whom wanted to be gang members, so I began to emulate gang members. I would study the way they walked, talked, dressed, their music, just everything. These were the people who accepted me, who invested time with me, and who gave me confidence.

By the time I started high school, I had changed schools 10 different times. I did not like high school, not because it was hard, but because I just felt I could not relate. Most of the kids were middle class.

I did not have the "high school experience." I did not care to go to dances or football games. I wanted a reputation, validation, and respect. Most of all, I wanted love and acceptance.

I started smoking and selling marijuana at age 14. Nothing major, but I thought I was Scarface. I did not make much money. I mainly did it for recognition. One thing about drugs is that they bring people together. I was introduced to new friends, and I tried anything that came my way: crack, cocaine, meth, and heroin. I did drugs not because I wanted them, but because they were always around the circle I ran with.

At age 16 I was fed up with life. I was always angry. Angry I was just a "wannabe gangster." Angry because I did not have a girlfriend. Angry I was always broke. Angry at my family for not giving a fuck about me. Angry I did not have a dad. I was especially angry at my mother. I found anger was more useful than sorrow because people respond differently to extreme behavior. When you throw all your "fucks" out the window, you become free.

I dropped out of high school my junior year. I dropped out because my friends made fun of me for going to school because I was missing the action. Showing up to continue school once a week was too much school. Dropping out of high school felt like the best decision I could make at the time. I was free to do what I pleased and free to pursue myself. I did not feel like a wannabe anymore.

Idle time is the devil's playground. I spent most days with my friends drinking, getting high, and partying. Loose women or "hood rats" were not an issue.

I was never allowed to have girls over nor did I have an example of what a "healthy relationship" was like. Everything I learned about women was on the streets. I did not have the whole boyfriend and girlfriend "meet the parents" courtship experience. I was the guy they sneaked out the window to see.

Always on the streets, I was never far from trouble. House parties would often end in fights or gunfire. I was shot at plenty of times before Afghanistan. I was finding trouble in the streets and with the law.

At age 18 I got an apartment with one of my friends. I was working at a factory for 12 to 16 hours a day, six days a week. My life was going nowhere. I was struggling to pay the bills. A lot of my friends were getting hooked on drugs or went to jail.

I was tired of the lifestyle I was living, and I was tired of the people I had around me. There was a parolee in his 30's sleeping on my couch whom no one wanted to hire. So his contribution to the house was to be our personal maid and occasionally deliver slutty underage girls to us. This man was a husband and a father. I did not want that for my future.

I always wanted six kids even before I knew how babies were made. My goal was to become the man my father never was. I could not accomplish that goal with the current lifestyle I was living, nor would I want to father any children with the type of women I was associating with. I needed to make a change fast.

JOINING THE MILITARY

I walked into the Marine Corps office with my face cut up and my knuckles busted from a drunken adventure the night before. "Why do you want to be a Marine?" asked the recruiter. "I wanna kill people," I replied. "You have a lot of anger. You will fit in well with the Marines. When did you graduate?" "I didn't," I answered. "Have you ever been arrested?" "Yes." "I don't think we can help you." replied the Marine. "Well, can I at least take the test?" I asked. He said, "If you want to take the test, I won't stop you. We haven't been able to get anyone to pass this month."

I took the assessment (ASVAB) the next morning and scored high. All my GT scores were over 100. The Marines placed me in night school and even tutored me in math. I would hang out at the recruiting office all day to stay out of trouble.

The gunnery sergeant of the office did not like me. I was bald with tattoos on my hands and the back of my neck, and my clothes were baggy. Sometimes I would show up with my friends who were covered in tattoos and usually reeked of marijuana. I was unable to see myself then.

I was interviewed by the Command of Marine Recruiting: three giant Marine officers who shark attacked me, interrogating me as to why I got into the trouble I did and the meaning of my tattoos. I ignorantly explained that I was a "G" from the hood and that they wouldn't understand anything about that life. I did not understand whom I was talking to, so it did not work out with the Marine Corps.

Working with the Marines for months meant I got to know the Army recruiters. It was easy to notice the difference between the two branches.

The Marines were a lot more uptight; everything was done by the book. They were united as Marines regardless of military occupational specialty (M.O.S.).

The Army was much different, much more relaxed. There was one soldier by the name of Sergeant Dang. Other soldiers seemed to be afraid of him, even those who outranked him. The Marines constantly talked shit about the Army. However, their tone changed when Sgt. Dang walked into the office. He had an "I don't give a fuck, don't fuck with me" swag to him. Sgt. Dang was a paratrooper who had just completed his second tour with the 82nd Airborne Division.

He became my recruiter and my friend. He was a Crip from Houston, Texas in a past life. He told me to stop going to night school and took me to a continuation school where he knew the principal. I was assigned a 10-page homework packet and was given 35 credits for completing it.

Sgt. Dang went to court with me, helping me resolve all the legal issues that kept me from joining the Army. He told me to burn off my tattoos. I did. Sgt. Dang also acquired other necessary paperwork I needed and got me into the Army.

I gave up a $10,000 enlistment bonus for an Airborne contract. I did not want to become an average soldier.

I'M IN THE ARMY NOW

I arrived at Fort Knox, Kentucky on August 29, 2005, to begin my five month One Station Unit Training (OSUT) to become a cavalry scout. They conduct mounted and dismounted reconnaissance, security, and assault. I was 19 years old.

One thing was obvious when I began basic training; there was a war going on. The Army was stretched thin and desperate to fill the ranks. The majority of the drill sergeants were activated reservists. The drill sergeants who were active duty had at least four plus deployments. As for the recruits, there were those who did not belong. They must have had some very shady recruiters.

There was McCoy, a hillbilly from Tennessee who scored an eight on the ASVAB. He must have spelled his name wrong. There was Macgyver, who was physically unfit; his feet pointed in different directions. This was his third attempt to pass basic training.

There were a few other criminals and petty thugs like myself who were wavered in. The majority of us were young kids. Our average age was 20, and we were predominately white and Hispanic, America's working class.

Kennedy, my battle buddy, was a good-hearted black kid. Before the army, the only interaction I had with black people were schoolyard or street fights. As a child, I witnessed gang violence between Pomona's north side (Mexican gangs) and Ghost Town Crips (black gangs). In the Sureno (southern Mexican) neighborhoods I grew up in, interaction with black people was a big "No." It took me a while to warm up to Kennedy.

In basic training, if your battle buddy is fucked up, you're fucked up. I had no choice but to drop my prejudice and learn how to work together. That's one

14

of my favorite things about the Army. The drill sergeants fucked with me a little because of my "cholo" (Mexican thug) demeanor and my "back on the block" walk. Other than that I found basic training disappointingly easy.

My fellow battle buddies liked me a lot. I was like something out of the movies to white boys from the country. They would constantly ask me about gang culture and life in southern California. I was surprised at how a ghetto Mexican kid from Southern California shared so much in common with a redneck from the South.

I was losing my ignorance. I had friends. I had a career. Most importantly, I was losing my anger. Instead of it controlling me, I was using it. Whenever I felt like quitting an event, I thought about those who wronged me. I mainly thought about my parents, and that rage pushed me through.

I found the personal growth I was looking for, and I was becoming someone unrecognizable to myself. After OSUT training, I attended U.S Army Airborne school in Fort Benning, Georgia. I loved Airborne school. Trainees were not being pushed through. Those who could not meet the standards were dropped. A typical Airborne day consisted of running and learning how to do parachute landing fall (PLF). This is done by jumping off a zip line and eating shit in a gravel pit all day. I completed my five jumps and earned my wings. Out of my class of 325 students, only 107 graduated.

Airborne school graduation was a proud moment in my life. My mother and paternal grandmother attended my graduation. This meant a lot to me because I always felt rejected by my mother and my family. As my mother pinned my wings on my chest, I thought, "You see mom? I am not my father. I am not a lowlife. You will be proud of who I become." Graduation gave me validation that I separated myself from regular soldiers or low energy ground soldiers (LEGS) as we paratroopers say.

I arrived at the duty station I requested, Fort Bragg, North Carolina, home of the Special Forces and 82nd Airborne Division. I can still feel the sense of pride and accomplishment I felt as I arrived at the gates of Fort Bragg. There was a huge sign at the entrance that said, "Home of the Airborne and Special Operations Forces." I finally made it to the real army.

The following morning my battle buddy, Mutuberria, and I went to turn in our orders to in-process. Inside the office sat two big and intimidating staff sergeants at their desks. Both had combat infantry badges (CIB) and Ranger tabs. While Mutuberria was in-processing, the larger of the two staff sergeants approached me and told me to throw my orders in the other staff sergeant's face and scream at him, "You better fucking help me!"

"Don't worry, I got your back," said the large staff sergeant. Reluctantly I did what I was told to do in the hopes that they would think I was cool. I could see Mutuberria's face of shock and fear as I threw my papers and screamed at the senior non-commissioned officer (NCO). I could see a look of disbelief on the staff sergeant's face as his eyes turned bloodshot red. "Get the fuck down!" he roared as he leaped out off his chair. The larger staff sergeant tackled him before he was able to get in my face.

I threw myself on the floor and put myself in the front leaning rest position. "Gotcha!" said the big staff sergeant as he was laughing hysterically. "Recover private," said the butt-of-the-joke staff sergeant. "Hey, brother, you're a pretty cool man, have a seat." I could feel the brotherhood as we sat and talked similarly to that of "homie love" that I felt in the streets, except this was real. For the first time in my life, I felt a true sense of identity. I am a paratrooper. I am the 82nd Airborne Division.

I was assigned to the 4th Brigade combat team 4-73 Cavalry Reconnaissance Surveillance Target Acquisition (RSTA). The 4-73 was a reactivated unit and was barely standing itself up because we were a new unit. We got the scraps of the division.

Our barracks were unfit for human habitation. They were infested with roaches and fire ants, and there was mold everywhere, so people started getting sick from mold spores. One-man rooms were two-man rooms, and two-man rooms became four-man rooms. We had spliced cable in every room and community gang bang showers. The only good thing about those barracks was that no one wanted to be in their rooms, which led to a lot of drunken community parties. We were moved out of those barracks after six months because someone's father videotaped the conditions we were in and sent it to CNN.

Pre-deployment life as a private was fun. I was never alone; there was always someone to hang out with. After growing up an only child in a single parent household, it was spiritually fulfilling to have the brothers I always wanted.

I was improving as a man in many ways. The anger was slowly being replaced by happiness. When I went home, I proudly wore my uniform. The family that was not in my life finally began to show interest in me. My father's side would throw barbeques for me, and since my father had burned all bridges, he was never present. When I came upon my old friends, I did not feel at home with them anymore.

Sometimes on leave, I would be counting the days until I went back. I missed my real friends. For the first time in my life, people were happy to see me. They didn't look down on me, nor were they intimidated by me. I still attracted "hood rats," but they were a lot hotter. I felt like I had made it. There was a bright future for me where my dreams of fatherhood and family could come true.

THE LEGENDARY
3RD HERD

I remember the first day I met Sgt. 1st Class Stephen William Jenkins. He walked right up to me and said, "I'm your daddy." He meant it because there would never be another man in my life that I would view in that light. He was a wise man who led by example. A good ole boy from Alabama, he had the ability to make you feel like a complete piece of shit without raising his voice.

Sgt. Steven Swanson was a tall, harmless looking white man who looked like the poster child of the Army. Looks were deceiving with Swanson. He grew up in North Las Vegas in an all Mexican neighborhood. Before 4-73, he was in 7th Group. He had deployed to Afghanistan four times.

Staff Sgt. Ortiz was from San Juan, Puerto Rico, and was quiet about his life before the Army. He had multiple scars that were not war-related. As an Iraq veteran, Ortiz knew his job inside and out. He was a great leader and fearless warrior and was a sight to see in a firefight.

Sgt. Richard Floyd was my first squad leader. He was new to the Army after serving 12 years with the Marine Corps. He was laid back and a great teacher.

Sgt. Aaron Pimm looked like a bully from a 90's TV show. He was from Canada, and his idea of fun was to go out into the wilderness with minimal supplies and survive. He was kicked out of Special Forces training with only language school left to go because of disrespect. Pimm was an Army Ranger who seriously didn't give a fuck. He was a great leader and remains one of my closest friends to this day.

Sgt. Henry Cancinos was a Mexican/Guatemalan mutt from Phoenix, Arizona. He came from the LEGS side of the Army where soldiers who were recycled in basic training are acceptable and weak physical training is the norm. He was unnecessarily overbearing at times, and most privates did not like him. To me, he was just another angry Mexican, and I bonded with him instantly. Sometimes you meet people you know will be in your life forever. Henry became the big brother I never asked for.

Staff Sgt. Johnson was a black man from North Carolina who was a reclass to cavalry scout. He was initially a tank crewman who was a very stubborn man and not the easiest to get along with. Johnson knew just as much about being a scout as his privates did. He was not a bad person; I think that cavalry scout was not the job for him.

The rest of the lower enlisted in my platoon were: Jack Gregory from Ohio; his sense of humor was unique and like a cartoon character. Tom Williams from Rhode Island; he was good at his job and loved shoes.

Brady Collins was from a wealthy family from upstate New York. The Army had the worst conditions he had ever lived in. Collins was a hard worker, but arrogant and looked down on people. The first conversation we had, he told me he did not like me for no apparent reason. I responded with a thunderous, "Fuck you!"

Braxton Black from South Carolina loved his biscuits and gravy. He was genuinely a good soul.

James Peterson from Phoenix AZ was loud, obnoxious and immature, but he was great at his job.

Daniel Hernandez was a big jock from Surprise, Arizona and we were roommates. He was Jenkins' favorite trooper. I was his second. We would jokingly call ourselves "Jenkins' Pet Mexicans."

Joshua Ben was from a small town called Sturgeon, Missouri. He was quiet, good-hearted, and everyone's whipping boy. We would eventually become the closest.

Ronnie Clark was a great guy from a loving family. He was from Savannah, Georgia.

Lt. Price, our platoon leader, was a moron and was replaced by Lt. Lawrence who was pretty cool for an officer.

There was something special about 3rd Platoon. We were the smallest in the troop with only 16 scouts. NCO's and lower enlisted are not supposed to fraternize outside the workplace, but we did. Swanson would throw barbeques on the weekends where he would make his famous "screamers," a secret family recipe for chili burgers. We would drink excessively and overdose on burgers.

Cancinos and I had a close friendship. During work hours he did not treat me any differently from the rest of the privates, nor did I treat him any differently, although it stung the most when he had to correct me. I respected him. Until this day, he remains a significant influence in my life.

Most of 4-73's duties in garrison were to be the 82nd detail assbitches. The first real training my unit received was at joint readiness training center (JRTC), located in the army's swampy butthole at Fort Polk, Louisiana where the opposition forces (OPFOR) are immortal. We trained to fight in the mountains of Afghanistan which were a complete 180 from the training I had received.

Since my first day in basic training, I was told I was going to Iraq. Most of my training was military operations and urban training (MOUT). On our downtime, we cleared glass houses. All of our NCO's, except Swanson, had been to Iraq. Swanson was a person other than grunt (POG) with the 7th Group. However, because he could drive the stick shift Toyota Tacoma's that Special Forces used, he was the driver on a lot of missions, so he saw more action than your average POG.

We used to make fun of Swanson because he had an involuntary twitch where he would shake his head and blink his eyes. I don't know if that is a side effect of trauma, all I know is now I have the same twitch. Swanson warned us that Afghanistan was no joke, however, I never really heard too much about Operation Enduring Freedom (OEF). The rest of our NCOs didn't seem to care.

We attended JRTC in October 2006 and were set to deploy in January 2007. I remember going on leave before deployment. It was a happy moment in my young life; I was proud of who I had become. I would wear my dress blues to the family functions which finally included me. I was a star among my lowlife friends, confident and secure with a paratrooper body and my mother's face. The "hood rats" took notice so hooking up was easy.

Since a young age, I was sexually deviant. My mother was scared for me based on her relationships and made it impossible for me to date

20

normally as a teenager. She put in my head that no woman would want me. I used to believe that. She took her anger against my father and men out on me. If girls called me on the phone, she would not give it to me. The one time I told her I had a girlfriend, she put every lie possible in my head. She harassed and manipulated me until I broke up with her.

I turned angry against women. In general, I felt all women were selfish, lying, manipulative whores. I rebelled. The only women I interacted with were on the street. I lost my virginity to a girl I met at a house party. I never knew her name. By age 17, I had my first threesome, and by age 20 I bought my first hooker on a weekend pass from Airborne school.

One time at Fort Bragg, I attended a wild party thrown by the wife of a deployed paratrooper (go figure). I had sex with multiple women, some of whom had just had sex with other men. When I sobered up the next day, I felt guilty. I had my friend, Jose Lopez, a spiritual man, pray over my genitals. I went to sick call the following Monday.

The line at the Fort Bragg STD clinic was the saddest, most pathetic line I have ever been in. It is a row of hopeless faces staring off into the distance. Getting "rodded off the range" at the clinic was a badge of honor. Damn near my whole platoon was rodded off the range. 1st Sgt. Sampson would always end the weekend safety brief with "wrap it up 3rd Platoon" (wear a condom).

I am not a fan of organized religion. As a child, my mother and I sought help from the Christian Church. Instead, they took advantage of us at our lowest point. I had always prayed growing up, and it comforted me the most when I was lonely.

After some time in the Army, I realized I was not the honorable man I had hoped to become. I was still very much a low life. What kind of honorable woman would want to settle down and raise a family with me? I made a deal with God that I would become a better example, or at the very least I would wrap it up saying, "If I don't live up to my promise then may my dick and balls fall off." That prayer will always bother me.

It was December 2006 when I was home on my final leave before deployment. I did my usual routine. I donned my ACU's, fatigues, visited friends and family, and smoked weed the first day I was home so I wouldn't piss hot when I returned. I visited my favorite strip joint called "Strip Joint" and met one of the most beautiful strippers of my life. Her name was Heather Lynn. She lived around the corner from where I was staying in Pomona. We had great sex the first night we met, and I remember laying with her looking at my dog tags shine in the moonlight. I couldn't be prouder of myself.

Returning to Bragg after leave was depressing. A lot of my friends were spending time with their wives and girlfriends. My roommate, Hernandez, was with his wife. Henry was with his wife. The barracks halls were empty. I called the stripper out of loneliness. I listened to her ring back song, "Put it in My Mouth," a long time before she answered, "Yeah?" "Sup, it's Jose," I said. She replied, "Yeah?" "Hey, I'm getting ready to deploy to Afghanistan." "Oh, yeah?" she answered. Click! "Hello?" I yelled in desperation.

I realized right then and there how meaningless my reckless decisions were. I'm about to go to war, and I have no one to comfort me. I compromised my values and broke my promises so quickly for a cheap temporary thrill. I was empty. "Everything will be all right," I thought. "I will go to war and return a better man."

AFGHANISTAN

We landed on a cold, snowy night in Bagram. I was surprised to be surrounded by tall mountains with snow covered peaks. I was so excited I finally got what I asked for, war. We were assigned our first forward operating base (FOB) at Orgun-East. The city was called Orgun-E because the eastside was all that was left after the Russians carpet bombed it. The living accommodations at Orgun-E were pretty good by Army standards. Joe's were assigned two-man rooms, and the chow hall, Hard Rocket Café, was good.

Orgun-E was rocketed regularly, but by the time we climbed up the mountain, the Taliban were long gone. This deployment is going to be disappointingly easy, or so I thought. Our time at Orgun-E was short, and the 101st Airborne deployment had been extended, so we went somewhere else.

Before we left, I had a conversation with a specialist from the 101st. He told me about a firefight his platoon had been in. They were ambushed by 100 Taliban fighters who closed within a few meters of his squad. He said, "We went black on ammo. We fought them off with grenades, and it lasted for hours." "This guy is full of shit," I thought. I never heard stories like this before. The news does not talk about Afghanistan like this.

FOB Wazikwa was located in the middle of nowhere. Living conditions were not too bad for an FOB with only burn shitters. (These are barrels of diesel fuel in which we defecated, and it was burned later.) We did 30-day missions from FOB Wazikwa which mostly consisted of me spending hours in a humvee on a turret-mounted machine gun as we wandered the barren mountains of Afghanistan. I preferred to be the gunner or dismounted.

One 30-day mission that especially sucked balls was when Price drove his truck into a muddy field in the dark after being told not to by Jenkins. His truck got stuck, and in our attempts to free him, all four of our trucks got stuck. Then the rain began, for weeks. We informed our company commander, Capt. Fulton, that the only way to get us out would be with chinooks. He called bullshit and sent 1st and 2nd Platoon to assist us. They all got stuck.

The rain turned into snow. I had to abandon the truck I was in because it started to take in too much water and sink to the left. We piled into whatever truck could fit us all in. We were stuck in waist-deep mud and snow. Fulton informed our Senior Commanding Officer, Lt. Col. Fields, that the only way we could get out was with chinooks. Fields sent in the infantry company to rescue us, and they all got stuck.

The rain and snow continued with the temperature below zero. We were five men crammed in a truck, cold and wet. Conditions were miserable. However, this was the most hilarious mission I have ever been on. Five men crammed in a tin can, miserably cold and bored, find ways to pass the time. The conversations ranged from describing every sexual encounter in detail to racial humor to hypothetical scenarios like what would you do if you were trapped on a desert island. We laughed all through the day and night.

When I tried to sleep at night, I would fantasize about the life I was going to build when I returned to the states. Would I stay in the Army? Would I become a police officer? I mainly thought about raising a family. The thought of my daughter sitting on my knee listening to the story of when daddy was trapped in the snow in Afghanistan warmed me up on those cold, wet, lonely nights.

When we had been stuck for a week, the villagers began to get tired of us. At first, they tried helping us by digging out what they could and trying to pull out the trucks with their tractors. It was no use. They were upset because we were burning their wood that they used for their "water machine." Since wood was scarce in Afghanistan, they began to steal our tools.

Ortiz had no tolerance for that. He began to scream at a crowd of Afghan men and threw one of them like a rag doll. A tool flew out from the crowd. Ortiz collided with the crowd like a bowling ball and then grabbed a teenage boy. "Navarro! Grab da fucking 9mm," shouted Ortiz. I was laughing as I gave him the gun and then watched him hold it to the boy's face. I held my squad automatic weapon (SAW) at the ready as I stared into the crowd of men who were begging for forgiveness. It was so easy to dehumanize them because we had nothing in common.

After nine days the weather got a little better. Swanson and I used that opportunity to dig ourselves out. We drove to FOB Kerkot Castle by ourselves. It would be another week before the weather improved and the rest of the troop could be pulled out by chinooks.

After only four months in country, I was sent home on R and R. I wasn't gone long enough to miss home or for anyone to care that I was back. I spent most of my R and R drinking alone, desperately trying to get laid by any means possible. I was alone. I missed my platoon terribly, and all I wanted was to go back. I thought being curled up nut to butt with another dude in the cold on some desolate mountaintop observation point in Afghanistan sucked at the time. However, being home alone with no friends and a family who could care less was worse.

I was only in country for a short time, so I had no crazy stories to share. The only combat experience I had at the time were rocket attacks, indirect fire, and a few improvised explosive devices (IEDs) that went off nowhere near me, nothing to brag about and no one to care. I took my mom and grandmother to Vegas for my mom's birthday. At least that was the excuse I used not to go to Vegas alone. I did this in an attempt to kill my loneliness.

I got a room to myself, donned my dress blues, and hit the town. "I'm going to be every woman's fantasy," I thought. "This R and R is going to be salvaged." Instead, I got drunk by myself, passed out on the dance floor, and paid a crack whore $400 for sex. I was empty. I missed my army family, my real family. I wanted to go home. I wanted to go back to Afghanistan. I wanted to go back to war.

When I got back to Bagram, time could not go by any slower. I was so anxious to get back. The 3rd Platoon hit their first IED without me.

When I finally got back to Wazikwa, Jenkins gathered us up and told us to draw a dick on a piece of paper. He then collected our dick illustrations, dug a hole, placed our cock art in it, set it on fire, and buried the burned drawings. He then stated, "I have to try and use my voodoo so we can stop getting fucked."

We were losing Wazikwa. We would be living in the field permanently, and only go back to various FOBs to refit after 30 days.

Sometimes our missions made absolutely no sense. Once we sat five miles outside FOB Sharona for 30 days in the same place.

Our Senior Commanding Officer (SCO) Fields, was not well liked by anyone. He did not lead by example. He stayed in the wire and walked and talked on his cell phone. At times our whole chain of command had no clue WTF was going on. This angered and frustrated me. When we returned to FOB Sharona, I called my mom complaining that I had no clue what was going on. We were just sitting in the desert doing nothing while the Taliban buried IEDs around us.

My mother called Rear Detachment (Rear D) and asked what her son was doing in the middle of the desert. This led to Rear D calling our command and told Jenkins that "Navarro was bad mouthing his NCO's". Jenkins, being the wise man that he is, told command no way Navarro said those things. "He doesn't even know the meaning of the verbiage you're using."

It caused a huge scene, but the whole squadron was called back to FOB Sharona and given hot chow. I received the worst ass chewing in my life by Sgt. Maj. Brown. I trembled like a wet kitten. Brown had a long talk with Sgt. Floyd, and Floyd stated that I went up the proper chain of command to find out what was going on. He himself did not know what was going on. Apparently, we were blocking a road denying the enemy freedom of movement. It sounded like something they pulled out of their ass, an excuse as to why we had no place to live.

I had been in country for six months, earned the rank of specialist, and not been in direct contact yet.

We were in Delia District when one of our trucks broke down. As usual, we formed a 360 perimeter with the trucks and prepared for the night. Our sleeping bags were out, we were smoking and joking, and I was in the heart of a breakdancing battle in the middle of a circle. There was a village about

26

a click away from us and ruins 500 meters north of us. What we could not see because of the flat dry landscape, not even with the long range surveillance equipment (LRAZ), was the huge dried out wadi, a dried out river bed, that surrounded us.

The Taliban used the wadi to encircle us. They were about 100 meters away when they opened up with rocket propelled grenades (RPGs), Russian machine guns (RPKs), and assault rifles (AKs). I began running to the lieutenant's truck to get on the automatic grenade launcher because none of us had our weapons or IBAs (body armor) on us. No one was pulling security.

I could see the rounds going between my legs as I jumped into the lieutenant's truck and climbed up to the turret with no combat helmet (ACH) or ballistic armor (IBA). I saw what looked like a football with an orange tail (RPG) fly about three feet from my head. I charged the MK19 automatic grenade launcher.

I saw a squad of Taliban in front of me, at least four of them, firing AKs, RPKs, and RPGs. I screamed, "Die, you haji motherfuckers!" at the top of my lungs so that everyone could hear me as I returned fire. I could see the rounds explode right where the squad of hajis were. No fire was coming from that direction anymore. "Fuck yeah!" I screamed.

Ortiz was on the LRAZ, laying on top of the truck bed firing away on the 50.Cal. He was fearless. He was acting platoon sergeant because Jenkins was on leave. He had no armor and no ACH, as he called for fire and communicated with every trooper while guiding our rounds with the LRAZ.

Cancinos was accurately lighting up haji with the MK19 while yelling in a Cuban accent quoting lines from Scarface. "OK, I reloaded!" he screamed. Haji surrounded us. We were getting mortared, crippled by a broken vehicle and terrain too tough to navigate in the dark. We had no freedom of movement. This was not the Taliban I expected. They were dressed in tactical gear and moving in squads with five-meter intervals.

After expending cases of MK19 rounds, silence fell from all sides. I ran to my truck where my SAW was so I could switch places with Clark, the forward observer (FO). Williams followed suit. Swanson was truck commander (TC). Hernandez was the gunner.

They had been reading magazines when we were attacked. Swanson returned fire first, hitting Hagi who were only 50 meters away. Rounds were coming through the turret as Hernandez climbed on the 240 Bravo. "I know I killed two motherfuckers by those ruins," he shouted. Ortiz yelled to Hernandez, "We got people running!" "Distance and direction," said Swanson. "We got eight motherfuckers by those ruins. Tag it!"

Haji sent a second wave. Williams guided the gunner's fire, and I was opening up ammo cans handing them to Hernandez. I was also recording the firefight and talking shit into the camera. Rounds hit the turret. It got stuck and was unable to traverse. Hernandez climbed out to fix it, and I climbed into the turret, grabbed Hernandez's M4 and began to engage the Taliban. We were winning.

The turret was fixed, and the guns fell silent. The Taliban then sent a third wave. We almost went black on ammo; only one ammo can was left. When the guns fell silent for the third time, Ortiz nonchalantly walked up to our truck and said, "Don't worry. They're gone. Great job everyone, but we cannot talk about the beginning. They can't find out we were fucking around when we were ambushed. Navarros lets go clear this fucking village."

Ortiz and I moved tactically into the village. Trucks followed. It was very dark, and I jumped at any shadow I saw. Ortiz grabbed me and threw me in front of him. "Go! I got you covered." I replied, "Fuck you!" "GO!" said Ortiz. With only the green glow of my night vision, focusing on the green laser dot of my PAC 2, we cleared the village.

The next morning it was like no firefight happened at all—no bodies, no spent shells, nothing. I accompanied the lieutenant and Ortiz when they talked to the laughing, lying village elders. We could see big piles of stacked hay, presumably where the bodies and weapons were being hidden. We found young men with burns and shrapnel, and dirt on their hands and knees. Due to rules of engagement (ROE), we could not search their homes or their compounds. It was infuriating.

I did not sleep that night.

The next day on our way back to FOB Warrior, Sgt. 1st Class Church's truck hit an IED. We stayed with the truck and pulled guard all night. The next night we were driving on Highway 1, and I had not slept in two days. I was in the dismount seat, Collins was the gunner, Gregory was the driver, and Staff Sgt. Johnson was TC. I had my IBA open, and my ACH was in my lap with my feet kicked up while fantasizing about a shower and hot chow. It was relaxing driving on the smooth paved road.

Then something snapped me out of relax mode. I velcroed my IBA and picked up my ACH thinking, "I should put this on." Before that thought finished in my head, KA-BOOM! An orange flash engulfed the vehicle with black smoke and slithered like snakes into my eyes, nose, and throat. An M14 smacked me in the face. I could hear everyone coughing in the black heat. "IED!" screamed Gregory. "No shit!" I angrily retorted.

We veered off the road and crashed into the only gas station in the middle of nowhere taking out one of the gas pumps. I got out of the truck gagging and coughing. Everyone was OK. Gregory was a little banged up.

I saw Ortiz's truck pull up, so I tried to act hard in front of him like I wasn't fazed, but it felt like I just got bitch slapped by a giant. The other trucks pulled up and dismounted.

Then I heard screaming and yelling, "Get the fuck up!" There were a man and a woman hiding underneath a motorcycle in a ditch. I could hear the woman sobbing a painful, terrified cry. "Shut that fucking bitch up!" I screamed. I took my weapon off safety and charged her. Ortiz grabbed me and threw me like a rag doll. "Navarro! Get the fuck out of here."

I walked into a nearby haji store whose window had been blown out by the blast. I opened up a box of mild 88's, sat down, threw on some 2Pac, and lit my cigarette. In the distance about five clicks away, I could see a firefight. I thought, "How did my little cholo ass end up in the asshole of the world?"

Up to this day, late at night, that woman's cry torments me.

The 30-day missions continued with long days of boredom and masturbation, wandering the mountains, IED after IED after IED. Bravo Troop 2nd Platoon lost Pfc. Jordan Goode. He was only 19 years old, survived by a daughter.

We were in Ghazni when 1st Sgt. Sampson, Capt. Fulton, and Sgt. Maj. Brown gathered us up for a platoon meeting. 4th Brigade requested a platoon to go to Camp Airborne, a small secluded FOB off Highway 1 located in the city of Jalrez, Wardak Province. They told us they chose 3rd Platoon because we were the best. It was a dangerous area. We would be joining my buddy, James Salazar's Platoon of 2nd Battalion, 508th Parachute Infantry Regiment. They could not hold the valley on their own. 1st Sgt. Sampson, the big intimidating man's man, was crying the day we left for Airborne.

The "3rd Herd" was more than willing to get away from the squadron and all its bullshit. We were going to be on our own as a family, running our own program. I was studying for the E5 board. I was already mentoring paratroopers, and we only had four months left of our 15-month deployment. I was happy. Life couldn't come fast enough. I woke up every morning hungry and ready to get after it.

We got to Camp Airborne, an old Russian base. The only structures that were not tents were an old building riddled with bullet holes and RPG blast damage, and the wooden tactical operations center (TOC), "the Rippenkroger War Room," named after Airborne's 1st wounded in action (WIA). Russian tanks (T-55s) and Russian armored vehicles (BMTs) were sprinkled all over Camp Airborne.

My buddy, James Salazar, was not there. He, along with 10 other members of his platoon, was WIA the week before. We saw their trucks shot to pieces and tires ripped to shreds. Inside, the trucks were covered in spent brass and torn, bloody ACUs.

We set up our tents. Hernandez and I stayed in the NCO tent. I set up Cancino's cot next to mine because he was on leave, along with Ortiz.

We got mortared our first night at Airborne. Nothing we weren't used to, but they got close, about 50 meters away close. Our FO Clark did his thing, and mortarman returned fire. A couple of days later when Swanson and I were on TOC duty, we were listening over the radio to a firefight Charlie troop was in. Then we heard killed in action (KIA) over the net. My friend, Sgt. Zachary Tellier was killed.

The next night we were called to a village just down the road. The Taliban had killed one of our FOB workers. The worker was praying in the mosque with his four sons, and the Taliban killed him along with three of his sons inside the mosque. They left the youngest alive to send a message.

I only caught a small glimpse inside the mosque before Lt. Lawrence shooed me away, but it was enough. The blood splattered walls and crying child over dead family members will stick with me forever. That experience made me truly grateful to be an American, thankful I didn't live in a country ruled by fear.

THE BATTLE OF JALREZ

The night before we rolled out to the village we had a platoon meeting. We were all nervous; too many guys got fucked up in that area. Jenkins assured us that we would be OK. We were going to roll in with Apaches. "They ain't gonna fuck with us cause we're coming in with so much ass," he said. He made it seem like we had the Enola Gay, Seal Team Six, and naval gunships on standby.

When we mounted up that morning, I could hear Peterson making fun of Joshua for wearing extra armor. We were told that our air support was scratched. My truck, Alpha Blue 3, included Swanson as TC, Collins as gunner, and myself and Blake and our mechanic as dismounts.

There was one way into Jalrez and one way out—a long narrow six-mile road. To the north of us were the mountains and to the south were huge dense orchards. All along the side of the mountains was spray painted, "Down with the US. Long live the Mujahideen" and "Death to the Infidels" in English. I had never seen anything like that before. It was intimidating.

It was a beautiful village, a rich one by Afghan standards. Children ran up to me and gave me apples. The whole village seemed to come out and greet us. I even bought a bag of popcorn for a dollar. I was not worried that something might happen.

"We had a leadership engagement with the Afghan army," a soldier told us as he pointed to the road. "You will be ambushed once you go around that corner."

On the way out of the village, it was a complete ghost town. It was eerie and frightening. A haji on a bike crossed the road in front of a convoy, no doubt a signal. "Look at that fucker on the bike," Swanson said over the net. "I see him," replied Johnson. "Keep your eyes open everyone," said Swanson.

I was scanning the road when I saw two curly white wires coming out of the road. I followed them only to see a haji at the end of the wires wearing a white turban covering his face before I could open my mouth. KA-BOOM! The truck in front of us, Ben's truck, was engulfed in flames. No way anyone survived that, I thought.

Two RPGs directly hit our front windows. A Dushka (Russian 50 caliber machine gun), or some kind of high caliber weapon, was lighting up the truck. The rounds were coming in as fragments, hitting Blake in the mouth. We sped out of the kill zone, but the Taliban set up interlocking sectors of fire along the entire route. These were not your average Taliban. They were concealed in the orchards and were shooting so close that our crew-served weapons could not shoot low enough, and were shooting from so high in the mountains that the crew-served weapons could not shoot high enough.

Collins was screaming that we had to go back for Ben. He saw him crawl out of the fire engulfed turret and fall onto the road. I could hear Jenkins over the net asking us if we could go back for Ben. We were stopped in the middle of a firefight cut off from everyone.

"We are pretty banged up over here," replied Swanson to Jenkins. As soon as he said that our truck lost power. "Oh shit," everyone said unanimously. A truck came speeding toward us. It was the quick reaction force (QRF) from the Platoon of 2nd Battalion, 508th Parachute Infantry Regiment. We waved them down.

With Blake shot in the mouth, Swanson looked at me. I ran out under heavy contact and tied our front tow strap. Haji were fucking everywhere, and it was raining RPGs and bullets from the top of the mountain.

Collins was still hysterical from seeing what happened to Ben and began to panic. Swanson was yelling at him to return fire, but he kept ducking. I grabbed his arm, "Collins, do you need a break?" I asked. "Yeah," he cried out, his voice trembling in fear. I pulled him down, asked for his shoulder armor, and casually put them on as I stood in the turret because I thought I was a badass. Yes, I was scared, but I was eager to get in the fight.

32

I felt helpless in the dismount seat as I watched hell on earth unfold. I engaged everything Swanson told me to. I could see the gunners in the truck towing us. One soldier was on the gun, and another was standing in the turret engaging haji in the mountains with an M4.

We came across another disabled vehicle, so the truck towing us began pushing it. We crashed into each other like bumper cars. As I slammed into the turret, I could see two hajis with AKs pop up. They were so close it seemed we made eye contact! I engaged them, and they dropped like flies. The crashing and shooting went on.

As I was traversing the turret, I heard a small pop like a black cat fire-cracker. There was a puff of gray smoke. I had fallen, and as I tried to stand back up, there was no response in my legs. I could hear Gregory screaming, "I can't see! I can't see!" I looked to the right of me, and I could see Blake passed out, badly burned, covered in blood. I could see pieces of bloody flesh all over the roof of the truck.

I looked at my hands. They were fine. I looked at my right leg. It was bent in a reverse L shape on top of the ammo cans. My femur was protruding out of my thigh. I touched the sharp broken point as I wiggled my toes. "Well, I lost a leg. No big deal, just my luck." I reached for my balls, and all I felt was burned flesh and blood. "Oh. Fuck. No." I screamed. My left leg was bent up almost to the back of my head. It was badly burned and smoking, pinned down by the radio mount. "Get it off," I choked out.

Swanson was bleeding heavily from the side of his neck. The RPG would have taken his head off if he had not dropped the hand mike just a moment before. That radio mount must have weighed 100 pounds plus, but Swanson pulled it off.

He was calmly giving commands to everyone in the truck. He told Collins, "Cover that up," and Collins covered my injuries with a fleece jacket. I could see the bag of popcorn I bought covered in blood. "Those cocksuckers got me for a dollar," I thought.

I was afraid I might live, so I was begging Gregory and Swanson to kill me. "We're all gonna die," Gregory screamed.

Swanson calmly told me, "No one is going to kill you, Navarro. We love you." He continued to give a situation report (SITREP) on the radio while an-grily yelling at Collins who was uninjured to get back on the gun. "No. No." Collins cried.

This is not a story of divine intervention or how to find God. What I'm about to tell you is absolute fact. I picked up Blake's M4, put the selector switch to fire and stuck the barrel in my mouth. I heard a voice from deep down within me say, "I got you." Simultaneously, I could see and feel the warmth of the sunshine coming through the trees from the windows of the truck. It was like everything stopped for a few seconds. I hesitated. I was ready to kill myself up until that point. Swanson knocked the M4 out of my mouth. "No!" I screamed.

Collins got back on the gun after Swanson attempted to get on it himself. The firefight continued. I tried to play dead, but Swanson kept checking on me, yelling, "Navarro" in my ear. I raised my hand and said, "Sup man?" I could hear my heart pounding. I was hoping it would stop altogether. The hot spent shells of the 240 were falling on me, burning my face as Collins stood over me. "This is it," I thought. "My mother is going to see me on the internet getting dragged out of this truck."

I picked up Blake's M4, held it at the ready on my chest and prepared myself for the inevitable. Then I heard the most terrifying sound of my life—it was the BURRRRAP of the A10 Gatling gun on our fighter jets. Even with two A10s strafing along the sides of the road, lighting it up, the Taliban continued their assault.

We arrived at the medivac site where Pfc. Pierce, our new medic, tried to help me first. "Don't you fucking touch me!" I screamed. As I began punching him repeatedly in the face, he backed up. I grabbed the M4 and jammed it in his chest. "I will fucking kill you!" I said sternly. I laid there on my back, weapon pointed toward the door. I was gonna fight them all off. I did not want to live.

I saw a tall white medic walking toward me with a big warm smile from ear to ear. I pointed the M4 at him, and he kept smiling, "Don't worry, buddy, everything is gonna be just fine," he said cheerfully. He threw me off kill mode. I was stunned at his demeanor given the circumstances all around us. I dropped the M4. "You're full of shit. I don't have a dick!" I replied. He stood over me, smiling and chuckling. I smiled and chuckled back.

More medics came and worked together to pull me out of the truck. The HALON system went off, so they were coughing severely. They tried to put me on a makeshift litter, but they dropped me. That was the first time I felt pain. My legs went in opposite directions, and I screamed a sound that I have never made since.

As they carried me to the bird, Jenkins walked next to me. I looked at him and said, "I'm sorry." I was still in soldier mode. "I should have just handed off the ammo and done my part. I should have never gotten on the gun." These were the thoughts in my head. I felt I had failed him. "Don't be sorry. I'm very proud of you. I love you," he replied. I was scheduled to go to the promotion board that week. "Am I a sergeant?" I asked "Yeah, buddy, you're an E-5," said Jenkins.

On the bird, Master Sgt. Dean Bissy was wrapping up my legs. He would later tell me that he was trying to keep my guts from falling out of the hole I had on my ass. Another medic, Sgt. Ball, was trying to put an oxygen mask on me, but I was punching him in the face. I still wanted to die. Ball put me in a choke hold and punched me three times in the face while screaming at me to shut the fuck up. I did, but he never succeeded in getting the oxygen mask on me.

Ben was to the right of me, badly injured. Collins was sitting behind me. He grabbed my hand and said, "Everything is going to be fine." I looked in his eyes with all the disgust and disappointment I had left. He knew right then and there how I felt about him. I could see it in his face.

I let go of his hand and turned away slowly. I was looking outside the bird at the farms. I could feel myself fading. The medics even covered my face with a sheet at one point, then uncovered it. We landed at Bagram, and people swarmed around me. I could only make out shadows, and I could hear them describe my injuries. My head fell to the side. "Yes, I'm dead!" was my final thought as everything went dark.

The next thing I saw was inexplicable. I was standing on the tarmac at Bagram, and everything looked normal. I could see the helos, the planes, and the mountains. The only thing that looked different was the way the sun shone. It was beautiful, and everything was completely quiet.

Then it looked like I fell face first onto the tarmac. I saw the gravel get closer, then complete darkness. I'm not saying I had an out of body experience. I am not religious. I could have been hallucinating the whole thing. At the very least, we can agree that that was some trippy shit.

Next, I woke up in a nightmare world. I knew I was dreaming and that I was alive. I knew something awful had happened to me. I saw humanoid creatures having orgies. I remember walking through a house where I could see women giving birth as demonic creatures ripped them apart. The floor was covered in mutilated baby bodies. I opened a door, and I was in an all-white room. My mother was sitting on a hospital bed. She was very sad. Even though I was dreaming, I knew she was right next to me.

WALTER REED

I woke up with a tube down my throat. I yanked it out and sat up to see all manner of IVs in my arms. To my surprise, my right leg was still there. It was in a metal vice grip looking thing. I was trying to take it off when I heard the crunching of plastic. It was a colostomy bag attached to my abdomen. I grabbed the bag of shit, and I started laughing uncontrollably, then passed out.

I woke up again to the sound of Happy Birthday singing. It was my 22nd birthday, Oct. 20th, 2007. My mother was there, along with my Aunt and Uncle Alvarez. They were the only ones from my father's side who made an effort to be in my life. I was happier to see them then I was my mother. I looked up to my aunt and uncle like parental figures. My mother and I put the fun in dysfunctional.

In the intensive care unit (ICU) the doctors came in and began to describe my injuries. They were not sure if they would be able to reconnect my colon. "How is my dick?" I interrupted. "Well, the head did not survive." "Well, that figures," I replied. "My balls? How are the boys?" "Those were gone in the initial blast," answered the doc. I definitely would have blown my head off if I knew that, I thought.

I could do nothing but slam my head into the bed and laugh psychotically, followed by hysterical sobbing. I cried every day for the next four months. I was overwhelmed. There were wound VACs, tubes that suck up extra fluid, on the lower half of my body. I could not see my injuries. My legs could not move. I could not grasp the concept of what was going on. All I knew was that I was finally able to sleep instead of having to pull guard all night.

37

I was operated on three times a week during in-patient. I was being transferred back to my room after surgery when Colin Powell placed his hand on my shoulder. "How are you doing, son?" he asked genuinely. I was in so much pain I could not respond.

Bedridden in the hospital, I started losing my mind. My mother had a bed next to me and was along for the ride. Any little thing would send me into a sobbing, blind rage. For example, there was a fly in the room that flew by my ear. My mother tried to swat it, but her hands clapping together made a popping sound similar to the RPG striking my truck. I lost my shit screaming, crying, shouting. My Mom just sat there looking at me and coldly said, "This is crazy!"

One night I was going seriously apeshit, so they called psychiatry. An Arab army psychiatrist walked into the room. "Get that fucking haji out of here!" I screamed. He sat on a chair in the middle of the room. "I will fucking kill you! Come here, you fucking Haji! I will kill you like I did your family! Fuck you!" I screamed at him. He continued to sit there and rub his mouth. His eyes looked cold and angry to me.

My nurse, Vasquez , came into the room and told the psychiatrist, "Dude, you have to get out." He got up and walked out of the room. I could hear my mother apologizing to him. "No, I understand," he replied.

Two years later Major Nidal Hasan would commit an act of terrorism killing 13 people and wounding 30 more in Fort Hood, Texas.

I woke up one night angry that I had to pull guard. I looked for my weapon and could not find it. I looked for Cancinos' cot. He was not there. "Cancinos! Henry? Henry?" I cried out. He was not there, so I tried to jump out of bed. The lower half of my body did not move, but my upper half fell out of bed yanking the IV lines out of my arm. A pain I have never felt before engulfed the lower half of my body. "Henry?" I began to weep. My big brother was gone. I was alone.

I felt the same emptiness and heartache that plagued me as a child. I will never see my little girl be born. What woman would want to be with me? I failed at the only goal I have ever set. At that moment Sgt. Navarro was no more.

I saw Ben as soon as I was able to. It took four men to gingerly lift me out of bed—half of my colon was gone, and so was my right butt cheek along with part of my lower left butt cheek. It was extremely painful to sit, but I rolled across the hallway to Ben's room because I wanted to see him. He was unable to speak because of the trachea tube in his throat. He was heavily medicated and half passed out.

Ben's wife was in the room. It was really obvious during our deployment that she was cheating on him, and the platoon gave him tons of shit for it. There she stood with a Louis Vuitton bag, coach shoes, and jewelry, perfect hair, and nails all bought with Ben's money. She was talking flirtatiously to a guy on speaker phone mode. How could this bitch have the audacity to do this as a human being? She continued her conversation in the hallway as I sat next to my brother staring at the stump of what was once was his right leg.

My mother encouraged the chore of me getting out of bed. She would pull me along with all my machines around the hospital. I was outside one day, and I could see the playground by the Malone House, an on-base hotel for out-patients. I watched a soldier in ACUs push his son on a swing while his wife was sitting on a bench bouncing their baby girl on her knee. I did not make a sound as the tears poured down my face, watching a life I always dreamed of, a life I thought I would no longer ever have.

FACING THE REALITY
OF MY WOUNDS

My next surgery was one of the most painful experiences of my life. My upper torso would be harvested for skin graphs. To quote the doctor as he prepared me for what was about to happen, "Have you ever seen an ice shaver? We are going to take one of those and shave your first layer of skin off your torso. Then we are going to staple Xeroform dressings to the harvest site. That's the only way it's going to heal." A mix of cadaver skin, along with my grafts, would be placed on my thighs and buttocks.

Recovery was slow and painful. Everything below my armpits and nipples had been harvested. The wounds seeped excessively. My arms would tremble because I had to keep them raised. It was too painful to put them down.

The lower half of my body was covered in wound VAC's. The severity of my injuries had not hit me yet because I was unable to see them. I dreaded the day when they finally did because that was the day I would have to face reality.

After another surgery, the wound VAC's were finally taken off. When I woke up, my pelvic area and my upper thighs were wrapped in gauze. I was wearing mesh booty shorts. On top of the gauze was underwear. I have held on to a few pairs and still have a lot of fun with them to this day.

Every couple of days students would come in and change my bandages. I was still too terrified to look down. After about a month, I finally got the courage to look down, and I was horrified. I began crying hysterically.

It was a whole lot worse than I thought.

FINDING HOPE DURING THE SURGERIES

For the first month at Walter Reed, I had surgery three times a week. My mother moved into the hospital room with me to help me out. It was the first time we lived together since I was 18. I loved my mother very much, but we did not get along very well nor did we really know each other.

Now I was completely reliant on her. She was my security blanket; I panicked if she left my sight for too long. She endured with me through the sleepless nights of beeping machinery and nurse visits. She was quick to tell the doctors to fuck off if they were disturbing me. I was spiritually, mentally, and physically broken.

One of my earliest memories of waking up in and out of my nightmares after being injured was the sight of Middle Eastern doctors. The irony was I thought I was shooting their cousins just the other day.

In the ICU, there were moments of complete peace as if I was asleep next to my friends in an Afghan Orchard on a beautiful day, only to wake up and realize the light I was seeing was not the sun but surgical lights. The voices I heard were not my friends, but the doctors and students poking and prodding me. I couldn't understand what reality was. I felt as if I was a car engine being put back together.

Different realities raced through my mind. Where am I? Am I in a firefight? Where is my platoon? Why am I here? Where is my Mom? There were moments of complete chaos. I was terrified, screaming and yelling incoherently. Sometimes I was restrained with straps on my wrist and sedated for attacking staff members.

Tom Vasquez was a combat medic turned Army nurse. He was an Iraqi veteran, so we clicked instantly. I affectionately nicknamed him va-jay-jay. Vasquez and I would spend all night talking. I shared with him my devastation, and we cried together. He did everything in his power to boost my morale. If a celebrity or anyone of importance came to visit, he made sure they came by my room first.

I was in-patient for several months when the boxing Super Fight between Ricky Hatton and Floyd Mayweather was taking place. It was a fight I really wanted to see, but I was stuck in the hospital attached to various machines. Vasquez took it upon himself to make sure I saw the fight.

Because his wife, Monique, was a nurse contractor working for Walter Reed at the time, Vasquez made sure she was my nurse the night of the fight. Along with other senior NCOs and officers, he gingerly lifted me out of bed with my wound VAC's super pubic bag and colostomy bag attached. They placed me in a wheelchair and smuggled me out of the back loading docks of Walter Reed.

We drove 45 minutes out to one of the lieutenant's house. It was the first time I had left the hospital since I arrived in October 2007. We hung out, talked, and drank like soldiers do. The combination of medication with alcohol had me on a good one. It was a great fight.

We returned to Walter Reed at four in the morning. My drunken nurses unloaded me from the truck, and we all laughed uncontrollably when the wound VAC on my ass opened up and leaked serous fluid all over Vasquez. We rolled down the hallways of Walter Reed giggling like schoolgirls and met up with Monique. I was smuggled back into my ward and did not go to physical therapy the next day because of my severe hangover.

That incident boosted my morale by placing hope in my heart. Thoughts entered my mind that life could be normal and enjoyable again.

THE HORROR OF REALITY

When the 4-73 returned from Afghanistan, I attended our Cavalry Ball in May 2008. It was bittersweet to be around the guys from my unit. Men who once looked at me with respect now looked at me with pity. Everyone knew what happened to me. it was embarrassing, and I was ashamed of myself.

I was awarded the Purple Heart and the Bronze Star Medal with Valor. Jenkins was there to congratulate me. He hugged me, told me he loved me, and that he would never forget about me. That was the last conversation we would ever have.

I brought a date with me to the Cavalry Ball. Sabrina was a girl I had pursued since I was 16, and was a street kid like myself. I fell in love with her the first day I saw her. We dated as kids, but nothing ever became of it. We never did anything past kissing. She was the only girl that wrote me in Afghanistan, and we had talked every day since my return. I explained that I was burned in my groin area but did not give her any details.

North Carolina was the first time we were alone together. She looked beautiful in the moonlight. After we were done being intimate, doing only what I was able to, I crutched my way to the restroom, colostomy bag and super pubic bag full of urine in tow. I stood in front of the mirror, took off my clothes, and pulled down the mesh underwear that held all the gauze around what was left of my genitals.

This was also the first time I looked at my naked body in front of the mirror. The horror of reality hit me. I shoved hand towels into my mouth to muffle my sobbing screams.

For the first time in my life, I was in love, but I could not make love.

43

"ACOCKALYPSE" NOW

I called it "Acockalypse" Now. I learned 39% of my body was burned. I was peppered with shrapnel all over. I was missing the majority of my right quad. My right hamstring was gone, along with my right butt cheek. Part of my left butt cheek was gone along with part of my left quadriceps. Both testicles were gone. My right femur was shattered, and my torso was harvested for skin grafts. I was urinating from a super pubic tube, and I was pooping out of my stomach. None of this concerned me.

I was worried about my dick.

The urologist at Walter Reed told me nothing could be done. If I couldn't handle the partial amputation of my penis, he said, "I was just immature."

My mother fought for a second opinion, and I met with Dr. Goodwin and Dr. Redford of Johns Hopkins Hospital. They create penises for people born with bladder exstrophy or other birth defects. I was impressed.

They build realistic penises with a procedure called a phalloplasty. They take a flap of fat from your forearm, and along with nerves, they wrap the flap around what remains. They attach nerves to feel erogenous sensation and pain. A penile implant is placed inside to achieve erections.

I was scheduled for surgery in June when I would be stable enough. To work on this gave me hope. I could not return home like this.

THE BUTCHER SHOP

In June 2008, I am 22 years old waiting in Pre-Op at Johns Hopkins, praying with my mother that a surgery that involves grafting a forearm free flap of fat to what remains of my penis would give me my life back. When I woke up after 16 hours of surgery, I could see Dr. Redford's tired face. "How big is it?" I asked. I looked down and was in awe at the master-piece he had created.

The monster that was now my penis seemed to be staring back at me. One million pounds of pressure was lifted off my shoulders. Not only did I look somewhat normal again, but I had also been upgraded.

The first thing I did on convalescent leave when I got back home in California was become intimate with Sabrina. With love, patience and a whole lot of lubricant, we were able to make love. I was in love with the woman I always wanted, and she did not care what was wrong with me.

My family finally recognized me. These things gave me hope for a chance at a normal life, a chance at love.

Testicular reconstruction would be the next phase of genital recon-structive surgery. First, they placed a balloon into what was salvaged of scrotal tissue. A port was placed so that once a week I could get an injection of saline into the balloon which would expand the skin recon-structing my scrotum. Once the expansion was complete, a testicular prosthesis would be placed inside the expanded tissue.

When I went back to Johns Hopkins to get this testicular reconstruction surgery and everything was finally done, it was bittersweet. Something was better than nothing, but I felt like a freak. Everything felt unnatural. The majority of my scrotum was scar tissue which made everything tight and uncomfortable. I was constantly tugging at my scrotum which added to my public awkwardness. I began to isolate myself more and more.

I spent all day in the Malone House hotel room. The only socialization I looked forward to was the smoking session at three in the morning with the other insomniacs of Walter Reed, where we went after surgeries. I think we all felt more comfortable at night away from doctors, nurses, NCO's, and civilians. Smoking and joking at night with other soldiers gave me a feeling of normalcy. I think the others felt it, too. During those smoke sessions, we were not injured. We were not patients. We were brothers. We were soldiers.

The crown jewel of my reconstruction would be the placement of a penile implant, which would be the engine that would make this freakshow work. It was my only hope to have normal intercourse with a woman.

Three years after being injured, I finally received the implant surgery. I had been on narcotics and antidepressants for several years at this point. I was drinking every day. I did not grasp the concept of what was happening to me. After the surgery, I felt worse. Implants were hard to the touch.

The harsh reality that I would have to live like this was stabbing me in the heart. Drugs, pills, and alcohol did the thinking and feeling for me. I was tormented by the fact that I was at Walter Reed against my will. I had to remain active duty to receive the proper care. I was never able to go home after Afghanistan. I felt trapped, surrounded by the miserable aftermath of war, living in the hospital.

I looked forward to my 30-day convalescent leave after each surgery. I could go home to California but always had to come back. In Washington, DC, I was isolated in my room. I had no friends. In my room, I didn't have to face reality. I could imagine myself to be whoever I wanted to be. Most days I just laid in bed snorting my prescription pills, fantasizing about how my life would be when all this was done. I spoke to my friends as if they were there. I replayed precious memories of Sabrina. I dreamed of California and the life I would restore.

The convalescent leave I spent in California would create memories that would push me through surgery and recovery. When I was home, I would stay with my Aunt and Uncle Alvarez. They still lived in the south Pomona neighborhood where I grew up. They never took into consideration that I was recovering from surgery.

They talked to me as if I was a child and gave me chores, but I didn't mind. I never had real parents growing up. Their house was warm. They sat and ate at the table like a family, something I never did growing up. Staying at that house, walking around the old neighborhood, gave me a sense of identity and belonging.

While home on leave, I hung out with the Navarro family. I had finally gotten the surgery I had always wanted, but I did not feel any better. Everything felt so painful and foreign. I was fighting a battle no one could see.

I had spent three years in the hospital with a total of one year in Afghanistan. After four years of not socializing with the outside world, I could not relate to anything anyone else had going on in their lives. Being around healthy civilians made me feel worse about myself. I could not interact with anyone unless I was drinking.

My surgery was fresh. I should have laid in bed for a month, but I was too eager to escape the cold imprisonment at Walter Reed. Given the psychotic medicated state of mind I was in, I did not truly grasp the concept of what was happening to my body.

The head of my penis was starting to turn black. Something was seriously wrong. There was no one I could go to for help unless I flew back to Baltimore. My grandfather Navarro passed away during my leave. I chose to extend my leave and stay for the funeral rather than seek medical attention.

I did not want to return to my cell at Walter Reed. Besides, I knew surgery would be waiting for me when I arrived. I was more interested in how the Navarro family looked at me. I was desperately clinging to them for purpose in my life, thinking maybe one day I could be the man for them my father never was.

When my leave was up, I returned to DC. The implant had eroded through the head of my penis. The pain was excruciating, and everything was removed . A malleable implant was placed inside my penis to keep the chamber in the phalloplasty open. My body rejected it. I woke up one morning to see a metal rod sticking out the side of my dick.

It had to be removed as soon as possible. That meant it had to happen in the doctor's office with no anesthetic. The doctor let me go to the liquor store and slam a bottle of Jack Daniels. I became so drunk I fell out of the taxi when I got home.

Recovery from the implant failure was far worse than the surgery. There was a giant tunnel inside the length of my penis. I had to stuff the tunnel with gauze, shoving it inside me with a long wooden toothpick similar to loading a musket with ball and powder. They do not make a pill for that kind of pain.

I would have to wait two years for the implant to be tried again. I began to spend months alone in my room. The only human interaction I had with someone other than my mother was when I would see my primary care doctor for medication refills.

Back at Johns Hopkins, Dr. Redford was trying to reconstruct my reconstruction that was damaged when the implant wore out. Urethra reconstruction is the most challenging part of genital reconstruction. They take a skin graft, roll it into a tube around the catheter, graft it to the underside of the penis, and leave it in for three to six weeks.

My urethra reconstruction was not going well. Fistulas would constantly form after surgery, and sometimes I would be pissing from four places at once. My morale was failing. I cut myself off completely from the outside world and attached myself to a whiskey bottle and pills.

Dr. Penski was one of my primary care doctors at Walter Reed. She was a young woman in her mid-30s. She took a liking to me, so my appointments would always go over time.

She was a good doctor who genuinely cared about me. She was also naïve, and I was a street-smart drug addict. I had a lot of affection and respect for Dr. Penski. She was like a mother figure to me, and I always looked forward to our time together.

Our relationship made it easy for me to manipulate her into giving me multiple medications. I always had a story as to why I needed more. I was able to see the conflict in her eyes and use it against her.

After so long, I wasn't her patient anymore. If I happened to run into her, she was very guarded and dismissive with me. I know I hurt her. Under healthy circumstances, I would've never done that to anyone.

RECONSTRUCTING MY BODY

One of the most significant issues I had with walking was stability. I was missing the majority of my right leg. The doctors wanted to cut off my left latissimus muscle and use it to cover the hole in my leg. I did not want to do the surgery, but walking was a painful chore. My sciatic nerve was exposed, and the slightest brush against a chair would be extremely painful.

The doctors placed my latissimus muscle on my right inner thigh to cover up a big hole made by the RPG blast. Before the surgery, it was just grafted skin over bone. The recovery was brutal, and I regretted the surgery instantly.

It was a surgery done by the Army, so Army care came with it. Against explicit instructions, the Army doctors forced a catheter into my reconstructed urethra which caused it to tear. The muscle flap covered up a big part of the hole but would require additional tissue expansions and surgery to cover the hole completely.

My sciatic nerve remained exposed. The muscle flap did not heal entirely. A fistula had formed in the flap. Blood and serous fluid were constantly leaking out of my leg. Attempts were made to close it, but it kept leaking. It bled for a year and a half. I woke up in pools of my blood. I would have to ring out my leg like a towel. This added to my discomfort of being in public. I spent my time in the safety of my isolation.

There was an external fixator that had been bolted into my bones to hold my shattered femur in place. Six weeks later it was removed, and a titanium rod was placed along the length of my femur so that I could eventually walk. It was replaced shortly after because of heterotopic ossification (HO), extra bone growth, that was tearing into my thigh.

During one of my next surgeries, to my horror, I woke up to the screaming death metal sound of Ooooh Whaaah! The doctor was blaring Disturbed's "Down with the Sickness" on a tape deck. The first thing I saw was someone standing over me, with hands, arms, and chest covered in blood. He was looking down, working on my leg with metal instruments. I was terrified and freaked out. I tried to roll off the table. "Hit him!" shouted the doctor. I could see the anesthesiologist pushing buttons. "Hit him again!" was the last thing I heard before passing out.

DOWN THE RABBIT HOLE

Back in the hospital, the surgeries continued and my colon was reconnected. At Johns Hopkins my urethra reconstruction was not going well. This is the most painful and difficult process of penile reconstruction. Walking, standing, and sitting was so painful there was a balloon inflated in my scrotum to reconstruct my nut sack. It was driving me insane.

In addition, my testosterone was grossly mismanaged. I was in constant torture, unable to sleep, and sometimes going five days with no sleep.

The stress began taking a toll on my mother and our relationship. She gave up her personal life to take care of me. We started our second year at Walter Reed with dozens of surgeries left to go. Then, the 4-73 returned to Afghanistan, taking with them my only friends.

After a yearlong relationship with Sabrina, things began to change, too. She became fanatical with the church she was involved in, and the leadership of her church did not approve of me. Sabrina swore a vow of celibacy, cut ties with me, and moved to Chicago to dedicate her life to missionary work. She did not grasp the concept of what I was going through even though we used to talk every day. She had been my support.

I spent the long, torturous nights in the hospital planning a future for us. That future left with her, along with my hope of achieving a normal life. Her departure broke the fragment of heart I had left. The pain of being blown up does not compare to a love lost. Depression began to set in.

In a final attempt to reach her I wrote her a letter explaining how proud of her I was for bettering herself. I told her how much she meant to me and that I wanted her in my life. I sprayed it with my cologne, enclosed some pictures of us, and sent it out. She never responded.

The only friend I had left was Ben. We lived next door to each other in the Malone House. It took a whole year before we were able to talk to each other. Every time we looked at each other, we were reminded of that day. Once we began talking, though, we were inseparable. His wife had left him, so all we had was each other. We usually spent the whole day together. We would always end the day with adult swim.

In June 2009, Ben's out-processing was complete, and he moved to Florida. I was alone again. I began to isolate myself more and more. With each failed surgery, I lost more hope. I went to psychiatry to seek help, but all they did was shove pills down my throat and encourage me to talk about Afghanistan. People who have never been to war have no business discussing or treating it. I never spoke about Afghanistan until I began psychotherapy.

Living in isolation like I was, Afghanistan was all I thought about. I was on a plethora of medication—Paxil, Kolonipin, OxyContin, OxyContin IR, Ambien CR, and Lyrica. I started to abuse my medication. I crushed OxyContin and Kolonipin, then mixed them together to snort along with a bottle of whiskey. I used anything to numb the pain and heartbreak.

The only reasons I got out of bed were to have surgery or buy alcohol. I would show up piss drunk to surgery. Sometimes I would take narcotics the morning of surgery in the hope that I would never wake up. To my disappointment, I always did.

When I was dragged out of my room to socialize, I behaved like an abused dog that had been locked in a cage. I wanted to hump, fight, and piss on everything.

Although I didn't recognize it at the time, people's expressions changed when they spoke to me. I was negative and vulgar. The content that I brought up in normal conversation was shocking and inappropriate. When you're isolated in your own little world without socialization, your thinking, actions, and sense of humor only make sense to you.

I could sense that people felt pity for me. They couldn't understand why a young man like myself wasn't married with children like all the other Mexicans.

I felt like screaming in peoples' faces sometimes, "I have been locked up in a butcher shop getting experimented on for years. There is a

52

medieval torture device implanted in my scrotum. You have no fucking clue who you're dealing with!"

I felt like a foreigner in my own home. I wanted to be with my own kind. I could not relate to anyone at home anymore. They did not understand me, and I did not understand them. No one could see my wounds, and nobody knew about the war I was fighting at home and within myself.

Physical pain does not hurt as much as loneliness, rejection, and humiliation. I was an outcast fighting battles on every front so that I could have a place in this new world.

People knew what had happened to me, so they would ask to see my new junk. I became famous at Walter Reed. I drank excessively. Although I could barely walk, I tried to pick fights with anyone, even those who were nice to me.

All I thought about was death. In my high rise apartment in downtown Silver Spring, I could see young couples having fun as I looked out the window. I could do nothing but cry as I sat alone in my room, in a puddle of my blood and serous fluid with a catheter sewn in my new penis. I was 24 years old.

The in-patient care at Walter Reed was great. The out-patient care was not. As soon as you're stable enough, they want to kick you out to the VA system. I was a specialty case. The doctors at Walter Reed could not treat me because of government regulations. They could not give me the proper dose of testosterone I needed. As a result, I was lethargic, depressed, and gaining a lot of weight, with no interest in women. The army did not know enough about people with my injuries.

My mother had to fight every time I needed a surgery approved. It added stress to an already hopeless situation. I slipped through the cracks at Walter Reed, held accountable to no one.

The squad leaders at Walter Reed are stationed there because they need to be near a hospital. My squad leader was suffering from severe PTSD himself, so he could barely look after me.

Life in the hospital was miserable. Every day I saw a new 19-year-old with his limbs blown off or horribly mutilated. The suicide rate was high.

You heard the horror stories of combat, along with the common stories of the deployed soldier that sounded like this: she fucked my brother and took the kids with all my money.

The horror I experienced in Afghanistan does not compare to the horror of the hospital. My only escape was going back home to California on convalescent leave to spend time with my new found family. However, the family that was not in my life growing up began to show their true nature. The attention and glory that came along with having a "hero" nephew began to wear off. To them, I was just a kid with a "free ride" that never had to work a day in his life. I was constantly harassed. "I'm so proud of you" became, "I told you so."

I made the mistake of trusting my Uncle and Aunt Alvarez to handle my financial affairs back home. They began stealing from me. In my heart, I knew what they were doing, but I did not care. I was so alone I would do anything just to have company around. I desperately clung to the shred of hope that life was worth living. All I wanted was to be loved and accepted.

They did not have my upbringing. They never knew how much having a family meant to me. They did not realize that they were my only joy. All of my injuries were covered up with just shorts and a shirt. My family could not see my genitals filleted open from another failed surgery.

My opioid use increased, along with my drinking, in the hope that my behavior would eventually kill me. I hung out with some of my old friends from the neighborhood. I ended up spending my convalescent leave in grow houses doing drugs and carrying guns, hoping and praying something would happen to me. I was miserably lonely. I was in such physical and mental torment all I craved was death.

When I returned to Maryland, I isolated myself in my room. It was my way of not having to deal with the outside world. My drug and alcohol abuse continued. I was in so much pain, yet inside I felt nothing. I would cut myself with knives in an attempt to feel something.

Alone in my room, I imagined a better life. I would think about Cancinos a lot. I would talk to him as if he was there and would pretend he answered back. I would look at old text messages between Sabrina and me and fantasize about our life together. I just missed the company of her. Alone in my room with drugs and alcohol, my fantasy world existed.

In the real world, I was a friendless science experiment. Complications with surgeries continued. Back home my aunt and uncle continued to steal from me. I felt so unwanted; I held loaded guns in my mouth as tears poured down my face. When I tried to pull the trigger, all I could see was my mother's broken-hearted face.

I ordered my mother to go away for the weekend so we could finally get some time apart. I assured her that everything was fine. I told her to enjoy herself and that I would not be answering my phone.

When she left, I drank four bottles of Johnny Walker Blue Label along with 60 pills, a mix of narcotics and sleeping pills. It was impressive how long I stayed awake before finally passing out.

I woke up two days later in a puddle of urine covered in shit and vomit. My toy Chihuahua was aggressively licking my face when I opened my eyes. My head was pounding, and I had the worst cottonmouth. I sat up and said out loud, "Well, I guess I'm not gonna die." I laid in the bathtub for six hours sipping bathtub water and continued to shit and vomit.

It was cloudy when I went outside the next morning. I stood on my balcony and stared at the trees. The clouds shifted, allowing the sun to shine through on the trees so I could feel the warmth of the sun. It was the same warmth I felt during the firefight when I was laying in pieces on the floor of my truck. I thought about the voice I heard say, "I got you."

THE DECISION TO GIVE LIFE A CHANCE

I had been at Walter Reed for five years. I was so caught up in mourning the loss of the life I once had, so overwhelmed with the things I could not control, I did not bother to fix what I could control.

I hated the fact that at one time in my life I was able to run 10 miles through swampland, and now I couldn't walk half a block without being in excruciating pain.

I decided to fix what I could, so I thought I'd start with working out again. There's only one way to eat an elephant—one bite at a time. This would be my first bite.

I found an old work-out video, "8-Minute Abs" and I began an exercise routine every morning. So there I was: fat, crippled, and nut-less, working out with the chick on the video. However, it started making a difference. I got stronger.

I bought a weight set. I realized that if I wanted to work out, I could not take medications, which led to a slow wean-off from the meds. As I got off the medication, I began to think clearly.

I decided to give life a chance.

I set small achievable goals such as: go outside today, say hello to some one, make small talk with a woman, or try to walk as far as I can.

I spent years locked in a room, and it took every ounce of heart I had left to make simple conversation. I was so nervous; I would tremble when I talked to strangers.

TRANSITION TO CIVILIAN LIFE

For most 26 year-olds, buying a home is a dream come true. To me, it just felt like another place to stay. The house felt empty. The only companion I had was my toy Chihuahua, Cali Love. She was the only female I had to cuddle with if she was in the mood.

I was by myself, exhausted by 5-½ years of hospitalizations, trying to piece my life together. I did not know where I fit in or who to trust. I was terrified to leave the house. I freaked out whenever the phone rang. For the first time in five and a half years, I wasn't around people who were horribly mutilated in some way.

I was embarrassed by my scars. No one had a clue of what I had gone through. Once I got cussed out by some lady for parking in the handicap spot. "Don't you know there are soldiers getting their arms and legs blown off in Iraq?" she yelled. "Well, they should have gone to college," I replied.

I did not know how to interact. I spoke with no filter, constantly saying rude or inappropriate things. No one understood why I was different. They just saw a young Mexican man with no wife and kids who drank excessively. No one wanted me around. I was negative and depressing. There were still years of surgery ahead of me.

Pomona had not changed. I felt like I came back to the same bullshit I endured in my youth — no friends and no family support. Civilians only looked out for themselves.

Sometimes I wished I was back in Afghanistan with paratroopers who put the needs of the team before themselves. Another battle had just begun for this exhausted soldier. I did not feel I had the strength to make it.

BEVERLY HILLS

arrived at Walter Reed in 2007, and it was now 2012. I was weaning myself off narcotics and stopped taking antidepressants all together after an attempted overdose. My thinking was becoming clearer and clearer I couldn't handle the hospital life anymore. I needed to come back into society. My med board at Walter Reed was coming to a close, so I bought a house in the historical Lincoln Park District in Pomona, California.

Given the state of mind I was in, any real estate agent could have taken advantage of me. Luckily, I was blessed with a realtor who was married to an army doctor. She also had a son who was an army captain who had been shot in Iraq. She was an absolute angel and found me my dream house.

I was out of the army now, but I was still undergoing surgery at Johns Hopkins. Another failed urethra reconstruction surgery happened again, making my urethra worse off than before. After the surgery, I broke down in front of Dr. Redford and his staff. "I can't live like this anymore," I said sobbing.

I decided to seek outside care.

I linked up with a non-profit called Rebuilding America's Warriors (RAW). I heard about them when I was a patient at Walter Reed. I learned they work with veterans only when they are out of active duty. Maggie Lockridge, a retired Air Force nurse, is the founder and president of the organization.

Maggie referred me to Dr. Norman Leaf, a reconstructive plastic surgeon from Beverly Hills. Dr. Leaf reconstructed my right butt cheek, so I finally had some cushion to sit on versus sitting directly on bone.

The surgeries continued. When Walter Reed took out my left latissimus muscle, the contour on my torso became lopsided. Dr. Leaf was kind enough to offer to fix it. I would have to lose weight for the surgery to happen.

Losing weight for me at the time was difficult because of the constant surgeries, testosterone mismanagement, and weakness in my legs. I worked hard to lose the weight, and Dr. Leaf approved the surgery. It would be done on the upcoming Monday.

The weekend before my operation, I visited my favorite marijuana dispensary to pick up supplies for the operation to come. I do not take narcotics even after surgery. I stocked up on edibles. One of the marijuana brownies I bought was powerful. It was strong enough for 50 doses, and I didn't believe it, so I tried it out.

I didn't feel anything taking the recommended dose of brownie, so I ate half the brownie. I was struck with a hunger that could not be satisfied. In one day I ate pancakes, bacon, sausage, hash browns, a double double cheeseburger, animal style fries with a shake, two medium size pizzas, a box of ice cream, a bag of apples, a pound and a half burrito Loco with two tacos, and a quesadilla.

When I showed up for surgery Monday morning, Dr. Leaf was furious. He was completely in the right. I could do nothing but stand there like the fat, slovenly piece of shit that I was. Luckily for me, Dr. Leaf performed the surgery anyway.

Maggie also referred me to Dr. Gary Alter of Beverly Hills, another a doctor who specialized in urological plastic reconstruction and who also happened to be Caitlyn Jenner's doctor. You may have seen him on Dr. 90210 or the E-network when he explained the procedure he did on Caitlyn Jenner.

It was interesting to visit my doctors on Rodeo Drive in Beverly Hills. My Pomona ass never expected to be parking next to Lamborghinis while watching the paparazzi chase celebrities. I remember sitting in Dr. Alter's office drinking my cucumber water. Across from me was a supermodel from Australia. Sitting next to me was a transgender person who was apparently in her early stages. Here I am this blown up solider. It was like the beginning of a joke. I had the same moment after my truck hit an IED. How did my cholo ass get here?

Money makes a huge difference in the quality of care. It can buy health. I was set up under private care with Urology of Virginia, with other doctors in Beverly Hills, and their surgery was a much more pleasurable experience. I was the only one in the room versus my experience at Walter Reed where there would be at least six of us in an assembly line awaiting surgery. Being surrounded by men with horrific wounds and amputations added despair to an already hopeless situation.

After reviewing my medical records, Dr. Alter looked at me with shock in his eyes and said, "What a fucking nightmare! Your genital reconstruction has not been done right." To be more comfortable and functional, everything needed to be overhauled. The re-reconstruction of my genitals began all over again.

The process began when my penis was split open, and a skin graft was placed along the underside. Then a catheter was buried and sewn in for three weeks so that a groove for my urethra would form.

The prosthesis that was originally placed in my scrotum was removed so that a tissue expander, a baseball-sized balloon, could be placed inside my scrotum. I had to drive out to Beverly Hills once a week to get my tissue expanded.

For two months, I was miserably uncomfortable and tense. I wasn't able to walk straight or sit without extreme pain. The pressure from the balloon caused me to urinate frequently, and sometimes it was painful.

I even got into a car accident after driving myself back from an expansion procedure. I was going through all this while at the same time trying to assimilate back into a society I had not been a part of in 7 ½ years. It's difficult to converse about anything with anyone about anything positive when you are in extreme discomfort.

I continued my reconstructive surgeries in Virginia and Beverly Hills. They relieved me of so much pain and fixed what Walter Reed and Johns Hopkins could not. After two years of corrective surgery, I was ready for my final genital surgery, the penile implant.

Thanks to Dr. Alter's referral, my final surgery, or so I thought, was to be done by Urology of Virginia in Virginia Beach. Dr. Ramon Viasoro, a urologist, installed an inflatable penile implant. This is by far the riskiest and most painful surgery of reconstruction.

This was not without complications. One of the cylinders that was placed inside my penis was positioned too close to the surface of the skin. It began to wear out. I had been through this twice before, so I knew there is no drug to combat that kind of pain. If the implant failed, it was possible that I would never be able to have normal intercourse again because of the complications I had in the past.

This was devastating to me. I couldn't have a repeat of Johns Hopkins. I did not know if I would be able to handle the situation.

I was flown back to the east coast and was transported by wheelchair. I could not walk because of the pain. Any misstep could tear my dick open. It took all of my Ninja focus not to lose my shit.

With the help of my battle buddies and those who cared about me, I was able to push through, making a full recovery after a grueling five months. Seven years of surgery, seven years of torture, seven years of fighting a battle all by myself was finally over. I was "functional enough," and I could live with it.

Seven and a half years of getting my genitals butchered were finally over

After I had sex for the first time after all the surgeries, I went for a walk. I contemplated my life, and I thought about all the pain, misery and isolation I had experienced. So much of it was unnecessary. For what? Pussy? Was it really worth it?

You're goddamn right it was.

So now what? Well, I guess I did what most people do after conquering impossible odds – cocaine and hookers, lots of cocaine and hookers. Thanks to dating apps like Tinder that take all the social skills out of dating, I was able to conquer my disability equivalent to a double amputee climbing Mount Everest.

It was surprising to me how great of a sex life I achieved. No woman seemed to care, and I'm not just talking about hookers either. Size does matter. Don't let anyone tell you differently.

I got into the mindset that there was no war. It never happened. I was just born this way. Call it delusion if you want to, but it worked. I realized that all these years the only thing keeping me from living a full life was the bullshit lies I told myself.

I accepted the fact that my life wasn't normal. The road I would travel would be different, and no longer would I try to fit in or live up to society's standards. I was going to do whatever made me happy. There was no reason I couldn't achieve my goals.

The healthier my body became, the healthier my mind became. I began to value myself and those around me. After a drunken cocaine-fueled night of debauchery in Mexico, I looked at myself in the mirror. I was disgusted. I just had sex with six of the most beautiful hookers Mexico had to offer. I was hungover, vomiting and shitting violently. I asked myself, "Am I really enjoying life?" The answer was most definitely, "Yes, yes I am."

However, I was not loving myself. "This is not why I am here," I thought.

THE BIG BROTHER I NEVER ASKED FOR

When I was a child, I always wanted an older brother to show me the ropes. I spent a lot of time alone pretending I had someone to talk to. I did have an older friend, Miguel. He was my best friend. During my childhood, he was sometimes my only friend.

He lived across the street from my grandmother's house in Pomona. My grandparents weren't moving every couple years like my Mom and I. Their neighborhood was the only sense of stability and identity I had known growing up.

Miguel was a smart, athletic, and popular kid. All the things I wasn't. I used to imitate Miguel, copying the way he dressed, his haircut, and the way he talked. I did this to the point where it drove Miguel to reject and ridicule me.

The truth was I was lost. There was no family or parent to guide me, and constant moving did not allow me to keep friends very long. I hated riding my bike home to an empty house with only my pets as company. I did not want to pretend anymore; I wanted to belong, to be a part of a group or family.

In the street, I met like-minded kids, and I tried to fit in with their friends and family. I did not want to be the "homie." I wanted to be a family member. I wanted an identity.

The thing is, in the streets, there's no such thing as friends. Most people are out for themselves, especially the company I chose to keep. It's all about getting over on someone. There is a lot of manipulation, confusion, and deception in the street mentality. I quickly learned that was not me. I was not a lowlife. I knew better.

The army is where I found my identity. It's also where I found a big brother, Henry Cancinos.

Henry was an overbearing combat veteran with two deployments to Iraq. I was a boot private. Henry is from Phoenix, Arizona, a state that is plagued with the dregs of California. That, along with my stereotypical cholo demeanor, made it easy for him to fuck with me.

He tried to avoid being my friend at first. It would be considered frater_ nization for a sergeant and a private to hang out. We were both Mexican Americans, Chicanos, with a stereotypical broken home background. I saw something in Henry that I recognized within myself. Both of us were angry people, but our hearts were big. We gravitated towards each other and connected easily.

The more I got to know Henry the more I respected and valued him as a man. I paid close attention to any advice he gave me, and soon he unex_ pectedly fulfilled the older brother void in my life.

It wasn't Henry's soldiering or leadership skills that impressed me. After all, he was a LEG—he had not been sent to Airborne School yet. It was his moral code, priorities, sense of honor, and foresight that he instilled in me, all benefitting me to thisday.

Henry lived down the hall from me on the third floor of our barracks, and I usually headed over to his room after work. It didn't feel like I was visiting a friend. I felt the comfort of family even on the days he punished us "privates."

Sgt. Cancinos' preferred method of torture was to make us do various exercises while carrying his beloved "tank round," a dummy round for an Abrams Tank that Cancinos always had at the ready. He affectionately named it "Mr. Act Right."

Both he and I understood that work was work and play was play. I never held any grudges toward him when he would yell at me or give me extra duty. All was forgotten after work hours. Some of our favorite activities to do together consisted of drinking and going to strip clubs.

Sometimes we would go straight from the club to morning physical training (PT) formation still heavily intoxicated, as did most of the paratroopers in Alpha Troop. Troop runs were the worst. The stench of alcohol sweat and liquor farts lingered in the formation, and it was not uncommon for troopers to run out of formation to vomit or shit in the woods.

When Cancinos and I deployed to Afghanistan, we truly got to know and understand one another. We were never more than a few feet away from each other most of the time. In the FOBs we would eat and shower together. In the field, we would shit together. We had many conversations atop the desolate mountains of Afghanistan. We watched shooting stars together and made wishes for material goods and big booty hoes. We constantly argued over who was taller. We talked and laughed until we ran out of words.

I told Henry that one day we would retire together and live in the same state. His response was, "Fool! I don't need you!" I could see the answer came from a place of anger and hurt. He had lost friends in previous deployments, so I didn't take it personally.

I didn't make that comment out of any affection for Henry. I just knew in my heart that I was stuck with this asshole forever. It was therapeutic to have someone to talk to about my dysfunctional upbringing.

We discussed our futures. I was planning to return home to Pomona and get into auto body work or possibly law enforcement. Henry would often counsel me against returning home. He would say, "That's where the bullshit started. Your family and friends are here. Your place is here." When I did get out of the army and returned home, I realized how right he was.

Fatherhood and family life awaited Henry when he returned to the states. He had married his long-time girlfriend and baby mama, Stephanie, before we deployed. Stephanie was raised in the Army. Her father was a retired Sgt. Maj. and her mother was a retired Sgt. 1st Class. She was just as sold out for the Army as Henry was, so she was a great complement to his life.

I was taken aback when I first saw them together because Stephanie is taller than Henry and stunningly beautiful. I didn't know my boy had it in him.

When I was isolated in the hospital, Henry was the friend I missed the most. I felt alone again pretending I had someone to talk to just like I did when I was a kid. I thought we would never have the same friendship again. I felt weak and emasculated, and I was too embar_rassed to come around any of my old friends, especially Henry.

During Thanksgiving 2009 when I was at Walter Reed, Henry, along with some other homies from 2-508—Fabian, Jared, and Javier came to pick me up so that I could celebrate Thanksgiving with them and their families back at Fort Bragg.

At this point in my recovery, I had just had a life-altering reconstructive surgery and was on 12 different medications. I was spending my days alone and had lost touch with reality. My thoughts and ac- tions only made sense to myself, and I was falling deeper into mad- ness.

Even though I was happy to see them, being around my old friends and their families made me feel more like a failure. Everyone had high expectations for me. They called me "Navarro the hero."

This was the first time I met Stephanie face-to-face. She was eager to meet her husband's best friend whom she had heard so much about. Everyone knew what had happened to me, so I felt embarrassed and insecure. I coped with alcohol and narcotics, which brought to light my true state of mind.

I was unable to have a coherent or appropriate conversation with anyone. We talked about subjects ranging from cannibalism to claim- ing that I was part vulture. To counteract my insecurities, I exposed my new penis to anyone who wanted to see, which made a lasting first impression on everyone.

I did everything to try and hide the fact that inside I was spiritually tormented. Although I hated being alone at Walter Reed, I was count- ing the days when I would be back in the safety of my isolation where the real world didn't exist.

Henry remained in touch with me the whole time I was in the hospital even though he deployed two more times. When I got out of the Army and returned to Pomona, Henry was one of the first people to visit me in my new home. It was comforting to have the feeling of family in my house be- cause Pomona didn't feel like home anymore. I had changed into someone unrecognizable to myself and blood relatives.

Henry and I did our usual routine of drinking, barbecuing, and other "wholesome" activities. We were sitting on my front porch discussing life, and I was lamenting to Henry the struggles of re-integration and the feelings of failure and loneliness that came with it. He comforted me with his perspective of reality. "Fool, you were in the hospital for five and a half years. It's going to take at least that for things to become normal."

The best advice is always the simplest. Those words stuck with me through my trials and tribulations as I battled life-altering surgery, while at the same time tried to learn how to socialize all over again and find my place in society. Henry was exactly right about the time frame. It took about five years for life to have some normalcy.

Henry is one of the handful of people who stuck with me through the good, the bad, and the ugly. He remains an influential force in my life today. Sometimes I still feel like Private Navarro looking for Sgt. Cancinos' approval.

I believe that one day we will retire together and become neighbors so that we may continue our conversations about life as we look up at the stars and make wishes for all things good.

A FATHER FIGURE

Reggie was my father's best friend growing up; I always knew him as Uncle Reggie. He was someone I always admired, someone who made it out of the hood. Reggie restored classic cars, and was from one of the most prestigious car clubs in the United States, the "Style Car Club."

When I was younger, Reggie would give me side work to keep me out of trouble. As a teenager, I was nervous around him because I wasn't used to being around adult men.

While I was in the hospital, Reggie restored my 1968 Impala Convertible. Working on that project gave me something to look forward to during those long years in the hospital. Reggie had witnessed what I went through with the Navarro family, and he saw I needed a support network.

His wife and daughters accepted me as family. I no longer recovered alone after surgery because they showed up to see me at home. I was used to everybody running from me. They didn't.

Style Car Club gave me friends to hang out with and a reason to get out of the house. Reggie encouraged me to date again, but I did not want to. What woman would want to be with a mutilated psycho like me? Reggie told me, "Man the fuck up and stop using your injuries as a crutch."

I spent one year at war and five and a half years in hospitals undergoing experimental surgeries. Interacting with women again would mercilessly show me how abnormal I had become. I had a new body and did not get a chance to develop like other people in their 20's by dating and socializing.

Socially, I felt abnormal after spending so many years alone. I was insecure, nervous, rude, desperate, disrespectful, obsessive, sexually frustrated, negative, and eager to please. I would try to explain what I had gone through, but nobody cared. I did not live up to their "hero" expectations. I was used, played, and manipulated. Angry and frustrated, I reacted psychotically. Women were weirded out or afraid of me.

I took every situation as a learning experience. I have an open ear and got advice from my angels like Reggie who showed up in my life to offer sound advice. I recognized where I was and tried to do better. Reggie's wise words replayed in my head each time, "If she ain't cool with it, on to the next one." So I did.

Slowly I developed my social skills. I took the principles I learned in military training and applied them to my daily life. Gradually I began building myself up to a full reintegration.

OPERATION PROPER EXIT

I received a phone call from Joshua Ben in February 2013. He asked me if I wanted to go back to Afghanistan with him and Pimm. Of course, I said yes, however, I was in no condition to travel to Afghanistan. I was recovering from another failed urethra reconstruction surgery.

But I decided to go.

I wasn't sleeping well, and I was taking a lot of narcotics. I was scheduled to fly out of Ontario, California to Washington DC, then all the way to Kuwait, and finally Afghanistan. When I arrived at the Ontario Airport, my flight was late. The only way for me to make it to Afghanistan was if I bought a $6,000 flight out of LAX to Frankfurt, Germany, and then on to Afghanistan. So I did.

I arrived in Frankfurt Airport and had a four-hour layover. I had been traveling for two days and had not slept in three. I sat at the airport bar and drank German beer. I brought up World War II with the bartender, made a few Nazi jokes, and bragged about being on the winning team, America.

He taught me how to swear in German, and then gave me a piece of paper with some profane German phrases. I felt great eagerness for the trip to come.

Shortly after that gift of time, the German beer blitzkrieg hit me with the full force of the Third Reich. I stumbled onto the plane yelling German obscenities. I collapsed in my seat and stared out the window as the plane rolled down the tarmac. I made it. I can finally get some rest. I popped two Kolonzapins and passed out.

When I awoke, four German paramedics were standing over me. They all jumped back simultaneously as if they were shocked I was alive. Apparently, I had passed out, was snoring, and wouldn't wake up. Two German police officers escorted me off the plane.

They pulled the plane over as it was about to take off, so all the passengers were furious with me. I ended up spending the night in Frankfurt, walking around town with my military backpack. It felt like people were looking down on me because I was American, but it brought me a strange sense of pride.

I flew back home the next day.

I got another opportunity to return to Afghanistan for Operation Proper Exit with Joshua Ben, but no Pimm. It was the best flight I have ever been on. We flew business class from D.C. to Kuwait, and I did not want the flight to end. We had movies, video games, candy, ice cream, a bed for a seat, and hot towels. I had never flown like this before.

When I arrived in Afghanistan, it felt so familiar. It was like I was back home. How could I feel so comfortable in a place where I experienced some of the most horrific times of my life? It was also the place where I had some of the best times of my life and grew the most.

It was rewarding to see the progress the country had made: paved roads, an organized army, women out in public with no burkas, and actual buildings instead of mud towers. We traveled all over the country to places I had never been before, smoking cigarettes with Ben.

Standing on the rock floors of the FOB brought back memories like the time I was promoted to specialist. My whole platoon lined up in two columns. Staff Sgt. Floyd placed my SAW at the end of the two columns. I would have to make it to my SAW taking on a gauntlet of punches from the entire platoon. I was definitely in for an ass whipping.

Thinking fast, I acted as if I was going to charge, then abruptly spun around and shouted, "Yes, Sgt. Jenkins!" The entire platoon turned around and stood at parade rest. Jenkins was not there, and I ran through the columns unscathed.

Ben brought up the time he accused me of stealing his wallet from our tent at FOB Sharona simply because I looked like a minority who would steal. The wallet was found, and Ben apologized for being a stupid hick. After that incident, we truly became friends.

When we visited a special forces FOB, it was exciting and intimidating being surrounded by Green Berets and Navy SEALs. They let us shoot various weapon systems such as the Carl Gustav 84mm recoilless rifle. I finally was able to shoot a minigun. Firing weapons on a makeshift range while watching dumb ass Afghans walk right into our sectors of fire gave me the warm, comforting feeling of home again like when I was deployed there.

After the range, we visited Camp Moorehead, an Afghan commando training base. It was a former Russian army base. A giant stick figure paratrooper painted on the side of a mountain with Russian lettering was still visible.

We were shown demonstrations of the Afghan commandos' capabilities. They had come a long way since I was there. We met the general of the Afghan army and the Afghan commando Sgt. Maj. He was a serious badass who had been fighting the Taliban since he was a kid, and had been shot eight different times. He also had been to every school the U.S. Army had to offer.

At the end of the night, we had dinner with all the head honchos of special operations command (SOCOM). It was an intimate setting. We sat around tables set up in a horseshoe shape for about 50 people.

The lieutenant colonel of SOCOM walked in. He was an older man, large and physically fit, and looked as if he was made from stone with a 1,000 yard stare. He definitely had a body count under his belt. His presence commanded respect, and the room went silent when he spoke. He addressed us each individually and listened to us one-by-one as we told our stories.

Morrison was a quad amputee, only one of four from the global war on terror. He told his story about being blown up, and then receiving a double arm transplant from a female donor at Johns Hopkins. I would jokingly harass him for hand jobs because of his female donated arms.

My story was to follow his, and I wondered, "How in the hell am I going to top that one?" So I started. "Well, everyone gets their arms and legs blown off, but have you ever heard the story of the bionic cock?"

I was compelled to tell the truth. I told them about the battle of Jalrez. I told them tales about my hundred plus surgeries. I described to everyone in the room my injuries in explicit detail with the pain and heartbreak that came with it. I explained to this group of soldiers how I felt each time a surgery failed. I expressed my feelings of shame and embarrassment every time I failed myself in reintegration.

I finished up my story with how much I love my life. Then I stood up, grabbed my crotch, and proclaimed, "Now I have this Frankencock that's dropping loads with the best of them."

Shock engulfed the room, and all eyes were on the lieutenant colonel as his stone face cracked, erupting in thunderous laughter. The room was given permission to laugh, and hysterical laughter engulfed it. It made me feel really good.

As I smoked my cigarette that night, I was reminded of a conversation I had with one of my mentors. He told me that I was here for a purpose. He had a vision of me speaking to thousands of soldiers. Given the mental and physical state I was in at the time, I thought there was no way in hell I would talk to an audience about what happened to me. Yet here I was doing exactly what my mentor said I would be doing.

As we traveled around the country, I stressed the importance to soldiers of checking on their battle buddies. One conversation with someone you can relate to could be life-saving. I ran into some old friends at various FOBs, and it was as if I had just seen them yesterday. I visited the casualty support hospital (CSH) where I was brought in the day of my injuries. The room felt all too familiar. They still had my medical records and X-rays from that day.

I felt a sense of closure as I walked on the tarmac toward the C-17 that would take us to Kuwait. I was leaving Afghanistan under my own power, not on my deathbed. Before I stepped foot on the ramp of the C-17, I turned and looked at the mountains on the horizon. They looked exactly like they did the day I almost died. I put two middle fingers in the air and shouted, "Fuck this place." Those were my final words to Afghanistan.

TRUE LOVE AT
THE RIGHT TIME

T he first time I laid eyes on Sabrina I was in the eighth grade. She was sitting at the lunch tables talking with some friends, and I felt as if I recognized her. It was only for a moment, but for some reason, the image of her face stuck with me for years. I saw her for the second time when I was a junior in high school. I wanted to talk to her so badly, but I had just turned 16, and I did not have any confidence or game. For weeks I watched her in the hallways walk to class. I was trying to build up the courage to introduce myself.

One day during lunch Sabrina was sitting at the tables talking to some friends just like the first time I saw her. I was trying to think of something to say, but nothing came to mind. Thinking fast, I threw a little ball that I was bouncing at her, and it hit her in the leg. I walked up to her and pretended that it was an accident. Finally, I introduced myself to the stranger I couldn't get out of my head.

We came from a similar upbringing. Sabrina lived in a single-parent household, and her father was a drug dealer. Her mother made similar life choices like my mother, and went through depression as well. I recognized something in Sabrina that I saw in myself. She was fucked up. She carried a lot of hurt and anger just like I did. I truly enjoyed talking to her or just hanging out. I never felt feelings like this before. I wanted her more than anything, but I did not know how to express myself. No one had ever taught me about women; my self-esteem was low. My mother's words that no woman would ever want me repeated in my head.

Sabrina was used to older guys who knew the game, who were about the party lifestyle and already had been to jail. Those things were measures of success in our world. That was a lifestyle I was barely getting exposed to.

Sabrina lost interest in me because of my lack of maturity. It hurt like nothing I had ever felt before.

I sat in the backyard of my roach-infested duplex in Ontario and cried. I prayed to God that one day Sabrina would be mine. I lit up a joint and listened to oldies about love lost.

I was 17 years old when Sabrina and I connected again. This time I was a little wiser and a lot cooler. I drove a midnight blue 1994 Cadillac Fleetwood. My head was bald, and my clothes were three times too big but creased to perfection. Sexy cholo was in full effect.

I was racking up plenty of experience with girls of Sabrina's type. I was not intimidated by her at all this time, except that every time I was around her I froze. I couldn't understand why I felt this way. She was the most beautiful thing in the world to me, and it had nothing to do with her looks or her hood rat attitude.

There was just something special about Sabrina that drew me toward her. At this point in my life, my only experience with women were drunken hook-ups at parties and casual encounters in the back seat of my car. I didn't have an actual relationship yet.

For the short instances I did have a girlfriend, I would always end up breaking up with each one in a matter of weeks because I was afraid of getting hurt. I felt that I wasn't good enough for anyone. Sabrina made it obvious that she liked me and wanted me to make a move, but due to my low self-esteem I failed to act, and Sabrina lost interest in me again.

This loss fueled my negative perspective toward women. I became angrier at life and myself for not knowing how to have a relationship. My anger controlled me, and kept me alone.

I was good friends with Sabrina's brother, Richard. When I would visit Richard at their house, my visits weren't really for Richard; I just wanted to see Sabrina, even if it was only for a moment. One awkward conversation with her would send my mind into overload. Her laughter and her smile would make my heart skip a beat.

In August 2005, I went off to join the army. Now and then I would still think about Sabrina even though we didn't talk anymore. I always regretted not taking it further with her. I have never felt that way about anyone since.

It was lonely in the army. I had my brothers to keep me company but I had no one of my own. I was 20 years old, and I had never been in love. I hadn't had a real relationship yet. Looking back, I realize I was hoping the army would be the solution to this problem by teaching me how to be a man.

One of the first things I did when I went home on leave was to visit Richard in full uniform, of course. Sabrina was there, and it had been two years since we last spoke.

The attraction between us was still strong. Looking at me in my uniform she nervously choked out, "Um, uh, nice ass." Then corrected herself and apologized for the comment.

She had changed. Growing up Sabrina was a party girl, the kind you don't take home to Momma. However, in this stage in her life, she had become deeply religious. Tube tops and miniskirts had changed to conservative frump.

Sabrina explained that she had taken a vow of celibacy and had no interest in dating anyone. She was set to go to her church's seminary school to become a leader in the youth ministry. I couldn't help but chuckle underneath my breath.

We went out during my pre-deployment leave. Sabrina brought a chaperone with her, to my dismay, who wouldn't let us out of her sight. It was frustrating. I was about to go to war, and I did not want to go without a proper goodbye.

Sabrina wrote to me while I was in Afghanistan. She was the only woman to do so. I thought about her during the cold, lonely nights in the field. I couldn't understand why I always had feelings for her. I even talked with chaplain Rodriguez about her during a mass he held for my platoon in the field. Everyone laughed as my ghetto ass expressed my feelings for this "bitch" and this "hood rat."

When I was in the ICU at Walter Reed, Sabrina was one of the first persons to call me. We talked almost every day. Conversations with her would numb my reality for a few moments.

I decided to invite her to go to the 4-73 Cavalry Ball with me in Fort Bragg. She was reluctant to do so because of her new-found faith, but I convinced her by flying her mother out with her to Washington D.C so she could feel comfortable.

The first thing I did when they arrived was separate Sabrina from her mother so that we could be alone together. I had been surrounded by balls and men's butts for a year in a country where they hide their women. Even though I was horribly mutilated and had a colostomy bag full of shit, I made my move. She resisted and told me that the only man she wanted to be intimate with was her husband. Fueled by the desire to see her naked, I choked out, "I love you." I did not realize at the time how much I meant it.

The next day some of my battle buddies picked us up and took us to the Cavalry Ball in North Carolina. I left Sabrina's mother in Washington DC.

When I was around Sabrina the physical and mental torment I was going through did not exist. I had never been in love before. I felt as if I found hope and a areason to live. When Sabrina's church found out about the Cavalry Ball, they punished her. They constantly harassed her about her relationship with me, which made her feel guilty and hypocritical. Sabrina believed everything the church told her.

The church provided a way out for Sabrina just like the army had done for me. It was an opportunity to get away from the dysfunctional lifestyle we were born into. It was also the only way for us to have a chance for an actual future rather than become another statistic.

Following the guidance of the church, she cut ties with me and shipped off to seminary school. That meant within a day, I went from talking to Sabrina every day to not hearing from her at all. Overnight she vanished from my life, and I did not hear from her for months.

I was devastated because it didn't make any sense. Alone in my isolation, I convinced myself that if I wasn't mutilated our relationship would have worked out. I felt so foolish for thinking that someone would want to be with a freak like me. I jumped to the conclusion that there had to be someone else in the picture, someone who was "normal." Imprisoned in my isolation, I drove myself crazy.

The only ray of light I had in my dark world was put out. The only woman I have ever loved was gone. I would not search for another. For years I tried to get over her, but no matter how hard I tried to hate and forget about her, she remained in my heart. I couldn't understand why.

Sabrina tried to come back into my life a couple of times over the years, but she was no longer the girl I knew. She had become very religious, and I would have to abide by the rules of her church in order to talk to her. I wasn't able to have a face-to-face conversation with her without supervision. There was so much I wanted to say to her, but I could not.

She had no idea what I had just been through. She had no clue how her leaving affected me. I found her to be fanatical and ignorant, blindly following orders from a cult. In Sabrina's eyes, my unwillingness to abide by the church's rules showed her that I wanted nothing to do with God, However I wanted nothing to do with religion.

I was tired of Sabrina coming in and out of my life, so I told her that I wanted nothing to do with her, not even friendship.

Time passed, and other women came in and out of my life. I chased the idea of a woman who I thought would make me happy no matter how beautiful, good, or bad they were. They were not Sabrina, and I loved none of them. Sabrina remained in my heart, and I couldn't understand why.

Three years passed since I last spoke to Sabrina. After eight years traveling the world performing missionary work, Sabrina returned home to California. While helping her mother clean the garage and organize boxes of paperwork, Sabrina discovered the letter I had sent eight years earlier. She had never received it. When she opened the letter, the smell of my cologne hit her, and she erupted into tears. "It's Jose!" she sobbed as she read my letter and held on to our pictures.

I was living in her heart as well, but she knew how badly she had hurt me. She had witnessed corruption in the church and no longer wanted to be a part of it. She had now learned the difference between God and the church. However, Sabrina had a mentor in the church, a pastor's wife, who was like a mother figure to her and was dying of cancer. Sabrina would talk to her about me constantly.

During one of their final conversations, Sabrina expressed her regret about the way she handled our relationship. She wanted to leave the ministry and try to rekindle a relationship with me. Her mentor told her to follow her heart and not to live her life with regret. So, Sabrina left her church.

When Sabrina had found my letter, it was confirmation for her to contact me. She was afraid to call me, so she sent me a text message inviting me over for dinner. I wasn't surprised; something had always told me she would be back. I texted her back and agreed to dinner.

Thoughts of vengeance filled my head such as, "I am going to murder her with my new weapon of 'ass destruction,' and kick her to the curb." Then Sabrina called. I answered the phone angry and confident. When I heard her voice, it was nervous and shaky. I was barely able to choke out a response. I had frozen up just like I always did.

We talked for a while. Both of us were awkward and rambling. After we hung up, I looked at myself in the mirror and said to myself, "You are such a little bitch."

Dinner was ready when I arrived at Sabrina's house. To my surprise we were alone. We hadn't been alone since 2009. She was nervous and kept repeatedly asking if I was seeing anybody. Times were plentiful for Jose; a relationship was the last thing on my mind. My thoughts of telling her to fuck off were trumped by her beauty. She had matured quite nicely over the years, so I sat down and listened to what she had to say.

Sabrina expressed her regret about the way she had handled our relationship. "If I could have done things differently, I would have, but I needed to get away from the dysfunctional lifestyle I was born into," she said.

I was 22 years old, coming back from a war zone and dealing with catastrophic injuries. I found looking for redemption from poor teenage choices and a broken home to be so petty. Those things were normal for people where we were from. However, at the time I did not understand where Sabrina came from or the dysfunction of her home life.

"God told me to let you go. He assured me that He 'got you,'" Sabrina said. God "got me." I was taken aback when she said that because "I got you" were the exact words I heard as I lay dying on the battlefield. Sabrina went on to say that at 20 years of age she did not grasp the concept of what I was going through. Following instruction from the church, she believed the only way for her to become a missionary was to cut me off. Her eyes were tearing up as she pleaded her case.

I couldn't help but feel the hurt I felt when I lost her, despite my anger and pride. I looked her in the eye and said, "I would have given you the world. I couldn't stand to be without you." Sabrina asked if there was any possibility for a future for us. I replied with, "We could talk." I planned to use her and be done with her. I made it very clear to Sabrina that church rules were not going to fly.

The first night that Sabrina and I were together was awkward. She was nervous and afraid like a teenage girl losing her virginity. It was obvious she hadn't been bull shitting me about staying true to her vow of celibacy. I tried to be angry with her, but I could not. All I felt was love. Our night did not turn out to be the snuff film I envisioned. It was awkward for me, too.

Sabrina and I had not been intimate since my injury. This was the first time we had "normal sex." For the first time in my life, at age 31, with reconstructed genitals, I made love. It was like we were living a moment we missed as teenagers.

Sabrina was no longer my 20-year-old girlfriend. She had grown so much as a person. She was loving and selfless and met all my needs without me having to ask. Sabrina had changed me so much as a person by just being herself. I was unable to stay angry with her; something had softened my heart. I finally understood my feelings towards her and why we lived in each other's heart. We were being prepared for each other.

Our relationship would not have survived my time in the hospital. I could not have been a man to her while I was addicted to narcotics and contemplating suicide. She would not have been able to understand or care for me while she was suffering from wounds herself.

This is another example of how I have always felt guided. Everything in life becomes beautiful and perfect at the right time. Sabrina and I have known each other for over 17 years now. We have a strong relationship and an even stronger friendship.

Life will give you everything you want, but you may not get it the way you expect to.

SAUL MARTINEZ:
MY GUIDE TO WARRIORS & QUIET WATERS

The first time I met Saul Martinez was at Walter Reed Army Medical Center. He was always smiling and greeting everyone. It bothered me because I thought, "What in the hell does this double amputee have to smile about? We are stuck here in this prison for freaks. How could he be so damn chipper?" It was impressive to watch Saul get around on his prosthetics. You would never know he was a double amputee unless his prosthetics were showing.

The second time I ran into Saul was during my participation in Operation Proper Exit. We were assigned as roommates. I had a lot in common with this jolly green giant because we were both Mexican Americans from Southern California, and both of us grew up about 20 miles away from each other.

During our time rooming together, Saul informed me he was the Director of Warrior Services for a nonprofit called Warriors & Quiet Waters. I learned this organization promotes recovery for wounded warriors through fly fishing in Montana. He invited me and my battle buddy, Joshua Ben, to one of their five-day FX's. (An FX is their military term for a fishing experience.) It sounded cool so we agreed.

The experience was so much more than fly fishing. The accommodations exceeded my expectations. I didn't expect to stay in a place devoted just to us warriors, with volunteers who cooked for us, gave us fly-fishing lessons, and guided us fly-fishing on rivers that looked like we were in a painting. I never knew places like this existed in America. The mountains and ponds surrounding the Warriors & Quiet Waters Ranch are so breathtaking, it is impossible to be in a bad mood there.

I met Cindy McCain during the close-of-ceremony dinner they offer at the end of each FX. She was a member of the Warriors & Quiet Waters national board and had come to meet some of the warriors who were attending. I was able to tell her that while I was in the hospital, my mother had brought me the issue of People Magazine with the McCain family on the cover. When I read about the conditions John McCain experienced while he was a prisoner of war, I felt inspired to believe I could endure what I was facing as well. His story meant a lot to me, and I shared that with Cindy. She and her husband's example were an inspiration for me.

She invited me to sit with her, so I did. We had a great connection because she is such a genuine person. Cindy advised me to keep pushing forward and told me that God had a great purpose for my life. She said, "When you realize that you are not in control, that's when you become successful."

During my second trip to the Warriors & Quiet Waters Ranch, I attended as a companion to another warrior. I was there to talk to, and fish with, another warrior, helping him to deal with his healing. I shared my experiences with him throughout the week, so he knew he wasn't alone in struggling with his personal battles.

I also spoke often with Mike McLeod, a former 82nd airborne combat journalist, who was there to photograph all of us in action. He is the most decorated combat photo journalist since Vietnam, and he's at the ranch for all the FX's to photograph us in action while we're fishing.

Mike wrote a book titled "The Brave Ones," describing his experiences during his tours. After our many conversations, he asked me if I wanted to write a book about my life and empowered me with the tools and guidance to write my first outline.

During my third visit to the WQW Ranch, I attended as one of the first participants in a CX that WQW was sponsoring, a Coaching Experience. When I came back to attend the CX, Warriors & Quiet Waters had connected me with a leadership coach named Ris Higgins, who just happened to also be an author and editor. Saul had matched us up for this CX, and neither one of us knew we both wrote, nor did Saul. She has patiently worked with me to complete my lifelong goal of writing this book.

I would have never interacted with Saul if I had not gotten kicked off the plane in Germany during my first attempt to return to Afghanistan with Operation Proper Exit. I would have never attended the second FX, which lead me to the CX, which contributed to me writing and finishing this book.

This is one of those examples of how everything happened for a reason.

FORGIVENESS

In 2017 Tyler Reece set up a small reunion in Outer Banks, North Carolina. Collins was there, and I did not know how I was going to react when I saw him. I told myself to follow my heart. If I felt rage when I saw him, then I should attack. If I don't, we would just talk it out.

Collins walked right up to me and said, "My man!" as he showered me with compliments. I could see the fear and guilt in his eyes. He was nervous to the point that he was shaking.

Collins brought his wife and child with him. I kept my eye on him the duration of the trip. I wanted to see the kind of man he was. He had his priorities right. He hung out and drank with us, but the needs of his wife and child came first. We were all hanging out at the swimming pool, so I pulled Collins to the side and told him, "We should take a walk."

As we were walking away together, I could hear Reece tell one of our buddies, "If Navarro comes back alone you need to help me pull Collins' body out of the ocean."

"Is there anything you want to talk about?" I asked. Collins broke down while he relived the events from the battle of Jalrez. "I saw what happened to Ben. There were so many of them, I completely froze. You stepped up and took the hit for me. There is not a day that goes by that I'm not tormented by it. Sometimes I just break down and cry."

Collins told me about his years of mental and spiritual torment. He was honest. He did not portray his actions to be something they weren't, or try to defend himself in any way. I told Collins that I forgave him. I felt satisfaction, so we hugged, and that was the end of it.

When I laid eyes on his beautiful baby girl, I felt a sense of closure. If I have to suffer now for her existence, so be it. I have a very happy life. As I watched Collins chase after his wife and child, I knew in my heart that his life was too simple for me. I wouldn't want his life. I wanted more.

We all went down to the beach later on that day. I stepped into the Atlantic Ocean. It felt as if I was being baptized. I shed the anger I had had for him and left it in the ocean. Looking into the vast ocean, I asked the higher power, "What is it that you want from me? Show me."

WHAT DROVE ME
TO SURVIVE

I am very fortunate to have people who loved me no matter how much I hated myself. I was constantly injected with love. No matter how dysfunctional our relationship had been, my mother never gave up on me even after I had given up on myself. All I could see was her when I held those guns to my head, when I popped those pills. I was unable to quit on her. In my experience, most soldiers who kill themselves do not have anyone to stick by them. Tragedy reveals those who truly care about you.

Growing up I always felt that nobody wanted me or cared about me. Now I have friends and family who are better than the ones I was issued. It is because of those people I was forced into loving myself. As I learned to love myself, I was able to love others.

Service to others is where I found my value. I learned I must become a man of value if I want the desires of my heart answered. Every day I try my best to grow my heart and my mind. I do not feel victimized. In my heart, I know that everything I have experienced in this life has been for a purpose. I can't help but feel that I have been led through every experience in my life. One thing I know for sure is that there is something greater than myself.

I spoke to a Navy doctor in Helmand Province on my return visit to Afghanistan in 2014. He said, "I have seen Marines come through here with minor wounds, and we think they're going to make a full recovery. Come to find out they die two weeks later of infection. We have also seen Marines who come in here as torsos and think no way in hell this guy is going to survive and if he does, he will have a poor quality of life. Come to find out they are living full lives. We are not the deciding factor. One day you're going to wake up and realize, 'Oh, that's why I'm here.' When you realize you are not in control, that's when you will become successful."

I have heard that exact same phrase multiple times from prominent people I have encountered in life, including the doctors from Beverly Hills and Cindy McCain. I am learning to let go and let God, if you will. Worrying about the future, questioning myself or trying to control things that are out of my hands, will accomplish nothing.

I know I'm here to accomplish something on this earth through every season of my life. I have been met where I was at. I had no father; now I couldn't ask for better father figures. I had no brothers; today I share a special bond with my brothers I went to war with, deeper than any blood relation. I had a poor relationship with my mother; now we are closer than ever. Gangs, war, over 100 surgeries, depression, PTSD, destructive behavior, and suicide attempts did not kill me.

Sabrina, the only woman I have ever loved, came back into my life. She is my wife now, and we make love constantly. Think about that for a minute.

I have experienced things in this life that I will never understand. Some of it was just plain cruel, but I consider myself lucky to have lived it. You have never truly lived until you almost die.

I live to the fullest, I love to the fullest, and most importantly, I am loved.

HOW I WAS ABLE
TO OVERCOME

As simple and corny as this sounds, I believe we all have that little feeling inside of us that is always looking out for our best interest. Often we don't listen to it because we don't agree with it or we just don't believe it. It's the feeling that comforts you in your darkest times, a feeling that gives you a sense that you're not alone. It provides the power that pushes you to your limits when you feel like quitting.

Sometimes we even blame that feeling for what's wrong with our lives. Have you ever screamed and cussed out someone who wasn't there? Have you ever turned your back or stated that you want nothing to do with something you cannot see?

There is a force that's greater than ourselves that cannot be explained. I first noticed it as a child. It comforted me when there was a hardship at home or when I changed schools again. When I found myself questioning a negative situation, I noticed it was then that I would be comforted with the feeling of purpose, thinking, "This is happening for a reason."

This is where faith comes in, and I'm not talking about religious faith. It's trusting and believing in yourself. It's listening to your heart. It's having faith that everything is going to work out for the best, regardless of the situation.

Do not let circumstances control your future. I believe adversity is the catalyst for personal growth. Loving yourself connects you to the energy that exists beyond your understanding.

Spiritual people often refer to the energy as God. Secular people sometimes refer to the energy as the unconscious mind. Whatever your beliefs are, I believe the power of this energy is undeniable. Connecting with it allows me to accomplish the impossible. It carries my burdens for me. It brings me the desires of my heart, as long as I remain connected to it.

My life is not easy. I live with mental and physical pain every day. Some things in life you just can't get over. I am not perfect. I will fuck up from time to time. I am not a role model. However, I am happy and fulfilled. I am receiving everything I have ever wanted, just not in the way I thought I would get it.

Having known true defeat, failure, pain, and loneliness enable me to understand and value victory. It allows me to love much more passionately and fuels the drive to push myself beyond my limits. It empowers my heart to heal my wounded soul so that I can give and receive love in ways I never thought were possible.

Luke 4:10– "He will guide His angels concerning you to guard you carefully."

GLOSSARY OF TERMS

240 Bravo	762 cal. Machine gun
A10's	Fighter jets
ACH	Advanced Combat Helmet
ACUs	Advanced Combat Uniforms, fatigues
AKs	Assault Rifles
Apaches	Helicopter Gun Ships
AT4 2-508	Platoon
ASVAB	Assessment
BMTs	Russian armored vehicles
CSH	Casualty Support Hospital
Cav ball	Cavalry ball
CIB	Combat Infantry Badge
Dushka	Russian 50 caliber machine gun
FO	Forward observer
FOB	Forward Operating Base
HALON	Fire suppressant that sucks the oxygen out of the truck
IBA	Ballistic armor (bulletproof vest)
ICU	Intensive Care Unit
Joe	Another name for Privates, i.e., GI Joe
JRTC	Joint Readiness Training Center
IED	Improvised Explosive Device
KIA	Killed in Action
LEGS	Low energy ground soldiers

LRAZ	Long range surveillance equipment
M14	762 Rifle
M4	556 Rifle
MK19	Automatic grenade launcher
MOUT	Military Operation and Urban Terrain
NCO	Non-Commissioned Officer
OPFOR	Opposition Forces
PAC2	Lazer dot site for night vision
POG	People Other than Grunts
PT	Physical Training
QRF	Quick Reaction Force
ROE	Rules of Engagement
RPG	Rocket propelled grenade
RPK	Russian 762 cal. machine gun
SAW	Squad automatic weapon
SCO	Senior Commanding Officer
SITREP	Situation Report
SOCOM	Special Operations Command
T-55 tanks	Type of Russian tank
TC	Truck Commander
TOC	Tactical Operations Center
VACs	Vacuum Assisted Closure
V device	Valor insignia
WIA	Wounded in Action

58518399R00062

Made in the USA
Columbia, SC
21 May 2019